PUBLIC UTILITY RATE MAKING
AND THE PRICE LEVEL

PUBLIC UTILITY RATE MAKING

AND THE

PRICE LEVEL

By

E. M. BERNSTEIN

Professor of Economics
University of North Carolina

CHAPEL HILL
THE UNIVERSITY OF NORTH CAROLINA PRESS
1937

PREFACE

THE GREAT DIFFICULTIES that have been experienced by public utilities commissions in regulating utility rates have to a considerable extent been due to the large fluctuations in prices throughout the greater part of the period in which the policy of administrative rate making by commissions has been in effect. In the decade prior to the World War the rise in prices was moderate and it was possible, although not without some difficulty, to make the necessary revision in utility rates. The tremendous rise in prices during and immediately after the war necessitated large and frequent revision of rates which could not be made satisfactorily in view of the general opposition of consumers. The short period of relatively stable prices in the 1920's relieved utilities commissions to some extent of the burden of frequent rate revision. However, with the sharp decline in prices during the recent great depression, difficulties were once more encountered. Consumers pressed for large reductions in rates, and utility companies faced with a decline in revenue from decreased sales resisted rate revision that would have reduced their net incomes even more.

Even the instability of prices would not have prevented effective regulation of utility rates if a satisfactory rate making method had been available. Unfortunately, the rate making rule established by the courts was too complex in its required procedure to permit the prompt and complete adjustment of utility rates in the period of rapidly changing prices. The ultimate purpose of the rule that utility rates must provide a fair rate of return on the fair value of utility property was to duplicate in the field of regulated rates the process of normal price determination in competitive society. Although it would have been desirable to regulate utility rates in a manner that would generally maintain equality of the prices of utility services with their costs of production, this was not in fact achieved under the rate making rule. With the complex, dilatory, and expensive rate making procedure

[v]

required under the rate making rule it was impossible to bring about prompt adjustment of rates with changing costs of production. Utility rates thus acquired an undesirable rigidity entirely out of harmony with the purpose of the rate making rule. The experience of the past twenty years shows conclusively the futility of attempting to regulate utility rates on the precise pattern of the price making process of competitive society.

Throughout the war and again in the great depression, commissions found it was impossible to use the rate making method and procedure required by the rate making rule. Instead, it was necessary to develop new methods of rate making that permitted the use of a simpler procedure under which rates could be adjusted more promptly to changing operating costs. The rate making methods developed during the period of unstable prices were designed to introduce greater flexibility in the rate making process, and for this reason they deserve consideration with other proposals for increasing the effectiveness of rate regulation.

It is the purpose of this study to show how the rate making rule and its procedure were developed, to consider the difficulties that were experienced under this rule, to discuss the new methods of rate making that commissions used during the period of rapid fluctuation in prices, and to offer a reasonable solution for the rate making problem.

This study of *Public Utility Rate Making and the Price Level* was undertaken at the suggestion of Professor F. W. Taussig. In his *Principles of Economics* (II, 118), Professor Taussig has commented briefly on the effect of the abrupt price advance during the war on the public utility industries. I have tried to carry the analysis into various aspects of the rate making problem during the war and postwar years and during the recent depression. The aid and advice of Professor Taussig have been invaluable in completing the study.

I should like to record my obligation to the Harvard Club of Chicago for the scholarship I held in 1927, and to the authorities of Harvard University for the Ricardo Prize Scholarship and the University Fellowship in Economics that I held in 1928.

Acknowledgment is made of the kindness of the McGraw-Hill Book Company for permission to use data on construction costs from L. R. Nash's *Economics of Public Utilities,* and of the kindness of the editors of the *Journal of Land and Public Utility Economics* for permission to use data on construction costs from an article by Professor P. J. Raver. The editors of the *Quarterly Journal of Economics* and the *Southern Economic Journal* have permitted me to make use of some previously published material. My colleague, Mr. Earl Hicks, has been very helpful in checking references and compiling the index.

E. M. B.

Chapel Hill
October 8, 1937

CONTENTS

PREFACE... v

I. THE RATE MAKING PROBLEM...................... 3
The regulation of rates—The unsettled questions of rate making.

II. THE RATE MAKING RULE.......................... 8
A statement of the rule—The fair rate making value—The fair rate of return—The Supreme Court on value and return.

III. THE PRICE LEVEL, VALUATION, AND RETURN............ 20
Fluctuations in prices and interest rates—Valuation at current reproduction cost—Valuation at prudent investment—Capital cost and rate of return.

IV. WARTIME REGULATION AND RATE MAKING............ 33
The objects of wartime rate making—The doctrine of corporate needs—Utility rates and the burdens of war—Wartime methods of valuation.

V. VALUATION: REPRODUCTION COST AT AVERAGE
UNIT PRICES 44
The prewar use of average prices—Five-year average prices—Ten-year average prices—The attitude of the courts—Some objections considered.

VI. VALUATION: THE USE OF CORRECTIVE INDICES.......... 59
Reasonable and normal appreciation—Corrective index valuation in Missouri—Corrective index valuation by federal courts—Disapproval of indices by the federal courts—An appraisal of corrective index valuation.

VII. VALUATION: THE SPLIT INVENTORY.................... 75
The split inventory method of valuation—The split inventory in New York—The split inventory in Wisconsin—The valuation of the railroads—The Supreme Court on the split inventory—An appraisal of the split inventory.

VIII. THE FAIR RATE OF RETURN......................... 91
The problem of rising interest rates—A temporary deficiency of return—A normal rate of return—Interest, dividends, and the rate of return—The Supreme Court on fair rate of return—Summary and conclusions.

[ix]

IX. RATE MAKING IN PROSPERITY AND DEPRESSION 105

The valuation question in prosperity—Fair rate of return in prosperity—The doctrine of reasonable worth—Corrective index valuation in depression—The rate of return in depression—Summary and conclusions.

X. A PROPOSED SOLUTION 120

Necessary changes in rate making—Prudent investment and capital cost—The New York rate making proposals—A solution to the problem—The prospect for the new plan.

INDEX 135

PUBLIC UTILITY RATE MAKING
AND THE PRICE LEVEL

CHAPTER I

THE RATE MAKING PROBLEM

1. The Regulation of Rates

FOR MORE THAN sixty years the people of this country have been struggling with the problem of regulating the rates for public utility services. In this time regulation has advanced from the passive and limited control of the early period to the active and extended control of the present. Legislatures, commissions, and courts have passed on the rate making question innumerable times, with the solution still far off. Progress has nevertheless been made. The machinery for regulating utility rates and the technique of rate making have been improved, the legal and economic aspects of the question have been clarified, and the problem is now limited to the determination of a fair rate of return on the fair value of the property used in producing the utility services. The facilities are at hand for a satisfactory solution of the rate making problem.

The right of the public to exercise some control over industries endowed with a large public interest was recognized at common law. For a time no active effort was made to regulate utilities in this country, public control being confined to the prevention of discrimination and similar abuses. The public interest was not recognized to be so great as to require extraordinary regulation. As in other industries, competition was expected to provide adequate service at a fair price. Rate making was left to the utilities, presumably on the theory that self interest would induce competing companies to maintain rates at the cost of producing the services. Where competition was inactive, the public looked to the courts for a remedy under the common law rule that rates must be fair to the consumer. In practice this remedy was ineffective, for the ordinary consumer could not undertake an expensive legal struggle for fair rates. It became apparent, therefore, that the regulation of rates through competition was unsatisfactory.

With the failure of competitive rate making, more stringent control was inevitable. The right of legislatures to determine the rates of industries with a large public interest was sustained by the Supreme Court, 1877, in *Munn v. Illinois* (94 U. S. 113). Legislative rate making was thereafter tried for thirty years, with the problem no nearer solution than before. Rates were drawn in the hurried confusion of a legislative session by men who lacked sufficient knowledge of the problem, and who regarded themselves as the representatives of the consumers. The difficulty of securing fair rates that the public had experienced under competitive rate making, the utilities now experienced under legislative rate making. From the point of view of the public this seemed to be an improvement, although it obviously was not the solution to the problem.[1] In the long run the public cannot have utility services at less than their cost of production. The fundamental fault of legislative rate making was in its objective: to establish low rates rather than fair rates.

At this point the peculiarity of the rate making problem in this country appears. In England, if parliamentary rates should be inadequate, the utilities would have no remedy other than to convince Parliament that in the long run the public interest requires rates sufficiently high to assure continued investment in these industries. In this country, however, utilities have another remedy. The Fourteenth Amendment to the Constitution provides that no state may deprive a person of property without due process of law, nor may a state deny to any person the equal protection of the law.[2] In a series of decisions, the Supreme Court has held that inadequate rates are in violation of these constitutional guaranties on property. This view, although al-

---

[1] On early legislative rate making, see S. J. Buck, *The Granger Movement.* A. T. Hadley in his *Principles of Railroad Transportation* holds the view that legislative rate making checked railroad construction in the 1870's. Low rates undoubtedly had some effect, but the chief cause of the decline in railroad construction at this time was the completion of the major roads. The depression of 1873 was also an important factor in limiting railroad construction in this decade.

[2] The Fifth Amendment places similar restrictions on the rate making powers of Congress, the Interstate Commerce Commission, and the District of Columbia Public Utilities Commission.

ready established, was well stated by Justice Brewer in the Texas Railroad rate case in 1894. "It is within the scope of judicial power, and a part of judicial duty," he said, "to restrain anything which, in the form of regulation of rates, operates to deny to the owners of property invested in the business of transportation that equal protection which is the constitutional right of all owners of other property."[3] In this and in other cases, the federal courts went beyond a statement that rates may be inadequate. They developed the principle that except in special instances rates would be inadequate that failed to yield a fair return on the property devoted to the service of the public.

2. THE UNSETTLED QUESTIONS OF RATE MAKING

Rate making under the Supreme Court's rule required the establishing of a fair value of the property used in providing utility services, and of a fair rate of return to be applied to this fair value. The determination of fair value and of fair rate of return was left to the consideration of the rate making authority, subject to the review of the courts. To avoid protracted and expensive litigation, and the danger that rate schedules would be set aside as confiscatory, it was necessary that the rate making power be delegated to a quasi-judicial administrative body, such as public utilities commissions. As the nature and significance of this rate making rule became apparent, such commissions were formed in all states.

It was thought that after commissions accumulated some experience, administrative rate making under the rule developed by the Supreme Court would be free from the antagonism and the litigation that characterized legislative rate making. Unfortunately, this expectation was not fulfilled. It should be noted, however, that unfavorable economic conditions contributed to the difficulties that commissions experienced in applying the rate making rule. The instability of prices and interest rates, the alternate periods of inflation and deflation since 1915, were important factors in preventing effective regulation of utility rates.

[3] *Reagan v. Farmers' Loan & Trust Co.,* 154 U. S. 399. See also, *St. Louis & San Francisco Railway Co. v. Gill,* 156 U. S. 649, and *Covington & Lexington Turnpike Road Co. v. Sandford,* 164 U. S. 578.

Nevertheless, in large part the failure of administrative rate making may be ascribed to the inadequacy of the rate making rule; and it is extremely doubtful whether further progress can be made in solving the rate making problem until this rule is modified.

The fundamental objection to the rate making rule is that the procedure it requires is unnecessarily complex, expensive, and time consuming. In 1929, after twenty-two years of commission regulation in New York, the chairman of the Public Service Commission of that state testified that "the commission has not the facilities to do the work that it is supposed to do with the efficiency that should characterize that work."[4] The primary cause of the ineffectiveness of utility regulation is that commissions are largely occupied with the difficult task of determining fair value and fair rate of return for many utility companies under the unsatisfactory rate making rule developed by the courts. There is not a state commission in the country that is adequately provided with the facilities and the funds necessary for effective rate making under the established rule.

Even under fairly normal conditions, with a moderate degree of stability in prices and in interest rates, the regulation of utility rates under the rate making rule is a difficult task. With the rapid fluctuations of prices and interest rates in the war and postwar period, and again in the recent great depression, it was impossible to regulate rates in accordance with the rate making rule, a fact that the courts were ready to recognize at the time. It was inevitable, under the circumstances, that commissions should devise new methods of rate making that came into use in many states. On the whole, these new methods of determining fair value and fair rate of return served a useful purpose, for they facilitated rate making in these abnormal periods, they showed the need for modification of the present rate making rule, and they indicated the nature of the changes required.

[4] Testimony of Mr. William A. Prendergast, then chairman of the Public Service Commission of New York, *The Report and Hearings of the Commission on Revision of the Public Service Commissions Law*, (*Hearings*, I, 31). The work of this legislative commission in New York is considered in detail in Chap. X, below.

It is unfortunate that with the return of fairly normal conditions, the courts have held that these new rate making methods do not provide the protection to utility property that the Constitution guarantees.

The rate making problem in this country is to devise a method of determining utility rates that will permit effective regulation, not only during periods of stable prices and interest rates, but also during those abnormal periods when the need for frequent revision of utility rates is greatest. A new method of rate making, to be effective, must be based on the experience that commissions have accumulated in regulation under the present rate making rule. It is the purpose of this study to show how the rate making rule and its procedure were developed, to consider the difficulties that were encountered under this rule, particularly during periods of rapid fluctuation in prices, to discuss the new methods of rate making that commissions used in these abnormal periods, and to offer a reasonable solution for the rate making problem. Unless the rate making problem is solved, and present methods of determining fair value and fair rate of return are modified to permit effective regulation of utility rates, the policy of private operation of public utilities under public supervision may have to be replaced by a more direct policy that will assure an adequate supply of utility services at fair rates.

CHAPTER II

THE RATE MAKING RULE

1. A Statement of the Rule

THE PRINCIPLE that utility rates must be sufficient to provide a fair rate of return on the fair value of the property used in producing the utility services was developed slowly by the Supreme Court in the 1880's and 1890's. It was not until the case of *Smyth v. Ames,* 1898, that the court made a complete statement of the rate making rule. The court said (169 U. S. 546):

> The basis of all calculations as to the reasonableness of rates to be charged by a corporation maintaining a highway under legislative sanction must be the fair value of the property being used by it for the convenience of the public. And in order to ascertain that value, the original cost of construction, the amount expended in permanent improvements, the amount and market value of its bonds and stock, the present as compared with the original cost of construction, the probable earning capacity of the property under particular rates prescribed by statute, and the sum required to meet operating expenses, are all matters for consideration, and are to be regarded in estimating the value of the property. What the company is entitled to ask is a fair return upon the value of that which it employs for the public convenience. On the other hand, what the public is entitled to demand is that no more be exacted from it for the use of a public highway than the services rendered by it are reasonably worth.

This is the rate making rule, modified and enlarged by subsequent interpretations, that commissions and legislatures are required to use in regulating rates.

In some states, supplementary legislation was enacted directing commissions charged with the regulation of rates to follow the rate making rule. Thus, in North Carolina the law provided that

> in fixing any maximum rate or charge, or tariff of rates or charges for any common carrier, person or corporation subject to the provisions of this chapter the Commission shall take into consideration if

proved, or may require proof of, the value of the property of such carrier, person or corporation used for the public in consideration of such rate or charge or the fair value of the service rendered in determining the value of the property so being used for the convenience of the public. It shall furthermore consider the original cost of the construction thereof and the amount expended in permanent improvements thereon and the present compared with the original cost of construction of all its property within the state; the probable earning capacity of such property under the particular rates proposed and the sum required to meet the operating expenses of such carrier, person or corporation and all other facts that will enable them to determine what are reasonable and just rates, charges and tariffs.[1]

It should be noted that whether or not state legislation specifies that the rate making rule must be followed in the regulation of rates, commissions are bound to comply with the rule under the Supreme Court's interpretation of the Constitution.

The rate making rule, it will be recalled, left unsettled many important questions. There was no statement of the manner in which the property actually used or useful in providing the services should be determined. Although various factors affecting the fair value of the property were enumerated, the court did not prescribe the relative weight to be attached to these factors in determining fair value. And nothing was said in the rate making rule of the manner in which the fair rate of return could be determined, or the factors that must be considered. It was probably the intention of the Supreme Court to permit legislatures and commissions to develop a procedure for rate making, subject to the review of the courts on the constitutional questions of due process and reasonableness of return.

2. THE FAIR RATE MAKING VALUE

In their rate making work, commissions have developed a procedure that is generally regarded as meeting the requirement that rates must be determined by due process of law. Rate schedules were changed only after a new valuation of the property used in producing the utility services. This valuation was made

---

[1] Consolidated Statutes, North Carolina, Chap. 21, p. 1068.

by taking an inventory of the company's property, to which was applied fair unit prices, and from which was deducted observable depreciation. The inventory was a detailed record of all property of the company used and useful in providing the utility services: land, physical equipment, overhead costs of acquiring or constructing this equipment, and intangible property.[2]

Land and physical equipment currently used in providing the utility services were included in the inventory without question. As for property no longer in regular use but still useful in emergencies, and property acquired in anticipation of future needs, a test of reasonable usefulness was applied. Such equipment could be included only at its value for its limited uses. From the value of this physical equipment, the courts have held, must be deducted the observable depreciation.[3]

The greatest difficulties arose on the inclusion of overhead and intangible items in the rate base. The courts decided that utility property involved more than the material and labor embodied in its construction. In undertaking a utility business, costs must be incurred for organization, for legal work, for engineering and superintendence, and for similar services not apparent from an examination of the physical property. These overhead costs, the courts have held, must be included in the rate base.

Three items of intangible property were in dispute: going concern value, good will, and the franchise. The courts have held that the business as a going concern is an additional property value to be included in the rate base; but that no special

[2] A valuation committee reported to the American Society of Civil Engineers that an inventory for rate making purposes should include the following items:

A. *Tangibles:* (a) land and buildings, (b) plant;

B. *Incidentals during construction:* (a) administration, (b) engineering and superintendence, (c) legal expenses, (d) brokerage, (e) promotion fees, (f) insurance, (g) taxes, (h) bond discount, (i) contingencies;

C. *Intangibles:* (a) good will, (b) franchise value, (c) going concern value, (d) working capital.

In fact, many of these items are not included in the rate making value.

[3] On depreciation, see *City of Knoxville v. Knoxville Water Co.*, 212 U. S. 1. Observable depreciation must be distinguished from ascertained depreciation as shown by records. The distinction is important, for reserves generally exceed observable depreciation.

value for rate making could be attached to good will or to the ownership of a franchise.[4] However, expenditures incurred in securing a franchise must be included among overhead items as part of the cost of organization. Although there has been criticism of the inclusion of some items in the rate base, the attitude of commissions has generally been that the question of what constitutes property used in the public service is, on the whole, satisfactorily decided.

The difficult question in determining fair rate making value was the choice of a method for valuing the inventory. The rate making rule prescribed the several factors regarded by the court as affecting fair value, and provided that they were "to be given such weight as may be just and right in each case." The classification of property in the inventory was a convenient basis from which to approach the determination of fair value. It was easier to reach a conclusion as to the value of a part than the whole of a utility company's property. Further, when a valuation was contested, it was the practice of the courts to require proof of the omission or under valuation of specific units of property. The findings of the courts on the methods of valuing specific types of property were more effective in determining the valuation method of commissions than the dicta stating the views of the courts on the theories of valuation.

In the valuation of land, it was decided by the courts that the basis for determining its rate making value must ordinarily be the market price of adjoining lands. In the Minnesota rate cases, the controlling decision on the valuation of land, the Supreme Court held that neither the original cost of the land nor the present cost of acquiring it for utility purposes was the proper measure of its value for rate making (230 U. S. 352). In the valuation of overhead and intangible items, two methods were widely used: the cost actually incurred and a percentage of the value of the physical property. Both methods were approved by courts and were used by commissions. In the valuation of physical property other than land, no satisfactory method of

[4] On good will and going concern value, see *Cedar Rapids Gas Co. v. Cedar Rapids*, 223 U. S. 655, and *Des Moines Gas Co. v. Des Moines*, 238 U. S. 153.

valuation was developed. It is in the valuation of this type of property, constituting the greater part of the rate base, that the greatest difficulties have been encountered under the rate making rule.

To find the fair value of the plant and equipment for rate making, fair unit values determined in accordance with the provisions of the rate making rule are applied to the inventory of physical property. The factors to be considered in determining fair unit values are prescribed in *Smyth v. Ames:* (1) the original cost of construction, (2) the cost of permanent improvements, (3) the par value and the market value of the stocks and bonds of the utility company, (4) the present cost of constructing the property. The first and second factors refer to the actual investment in the property. The third factor, the par value and market value of the securities, cannot be used in determining unit values, although these values may be useful in checking the results as shown by the final total value. The fourth factor refers to the cost of reproducing the identical property under original conditions but at present prices.

The rate making rule thus prescribes only two basic factors to be considered in determining fair value: the investment cost, and the reproduction cost. The Supreme Court said nothing regarding the weight to be given to each of these factors beyond a general caution that fair and just weight be given in each case. In practice, commissions found that the best way to make certain that a valuation would be acceptable to the courts was to compromise by taking a sum somewhere between the original cost and the present reproduction cost as the fair rate making value. The avoidance of litigation with its distractive effect on administrative duties was so important to commissions that any reasonable compromise seemed justified. The absence of a definite formula for combining the factors affecting fair value also made it difficult for the lower courts to determine with certainty whether the requirements of the rate making rule had been met. Where rates were too low to yield a fair return under either method of valuation, the denial of constitutional rights was obvious. But the issue was seldom so clear, particularly after the development of the present complex rate making procedure.

3. THE FAIR RATE OF RETURN

In determining the rate schedule for a utility company, the fair rate of return is as important a factor as ,the fair value, for the just compensation that the rate schedule must provide is the product of the fair value and the fair rate of return. Nevertheless, the differences between the utility companies and the commissions have been largely concerned with the question of valuation. There are probably three important reasons for this: first, the greater complexity of the process of determining fair value as compared with the determining of fair rate of return; second, the greater variability of the price level as compared with interest rates; third, the closer relationship of depreciation allowance to fair value than to fair rate of return. It is not to be assumed from this, of course, that no difficulties have been encountered in determining the fair rate of return on utility property. On the contrary, the question has been very difficult, particularly during the recent depression.

The underlying principle of the fair rate of return—that it must be sufficient, when applied to the fair value, to induce a continued and adequate supply of capital to enter the utility industries—was stated in the early rate cases. Even before the rate making rule had been formulated in 1898, the federal courts, including the Supreme Court, had recognized that a fair rate of return was associated with the need for additional capital in the expanding utility industries. How this fair rate of return could be determined precisely, the courts did not indicate, the question being left to the determination of the rate making authorities. But this the courts did decide: that the fair rate of return varied from place to place, from time to time, and in different utility industries. Ultimately the determination of a fair rate of return was a matter of judgment, and therefore not capable of precise formulation.[5]

---

[5] See particularly, *Reagan v. Farmers' Loan & Trust Co.*, 154 U. S. 362, and *Willcox v. Consolidated Gas Co.*, 212 U. S. 19.

The various factors affecting the fair rate of return were slowly recognized by the commissions and the courts. It was noted that the principal factor was the interest rate as shown by the yield on equivalent investments. The interest rate, however, could not be regarded as the sole factor affecting the fair rate of return, particularly as utility companies differed in many important respects. If the net return was to be compensatory under varying conditions of risk and efficiency, these differences had to be taken into consideration. The policy of the Idaho Commission on this question was typical. "The rate of return in each case," it said, "shall be determined after due consideration of the hazard and risk connected with the operation of the utility, the efficiency in operation and economy in management, giving to the utility showing the highest efficiency in operation and the greatest economy in management, and furnishing service to the consumer at the lowest possible cost, the highest rate of return."[6] In considering the fairness of the rate of return, courts and commissions took into account the interest rate, the risk, and the efficiency and economy of management.

The greater part of the fair return that was allowed to utility companies was regarded as interest on the capital investment. It was logical, therefore, that the factor given greatest consideration in determining the fair rate of return was the current yield on sound investments. Differences and changes in the interest rate were regarded as requiring differences and changes in the fair rate of return. Thus, the interest rate, and therefore the fair rate of return, was lower in the East than in the South and West. The rising interest rates of the first two decades of this century were regarded as requiring corresponding increases in the fair rate of return. It should be noted that the weight attached to the interest rate as a factor affecting the fair rate of return differed in various states. In general, the interest rate was given greater weight in the East, where it constituted about

[6] *Taylor v. Northwest Light & Water Co.,* Public Utility Reports (hereafter cited as P. U. R.) 1916 A, 372. Compare the six factors considered by the Missouri Commission: the amount of investment, the stability of investment, successful operation, competition, risk, interest on borrowed money. *Re Kansas City Electric Light Co.,* P. U. R. 1917 C, 728.

three-fourths of the fair rate of return, than in the West, where it constituted about three-fifths of the fair rate of return.

The risk factor was given exceptionally great weight in the Mountain States. Risks were regarded as of three main types: those associated with the utility, with the community, and with competition. The fair rate of return was held to be lower for such utilities as water works and telephone companies than for such unusually hazardous enterprises as natural gas, bridges, and ferries. The risks associated with communities were subject to great variation. In mining communities a relatively high rate of return was not regarded as excessive, largely because of the great risk of shifting population. On the other hand, in cities such as New York and Chicago, where the demand for utility services was not subject to great or sudden variation, a relatively low rate of return was regarded as fair. The risks associated with actual or potential competition were not great for most utility companies; but where such risks did prevail a higher rate of return was generally allowed.[7]

The third major factor given consideration in determining fair rate of return was the efficiency and economy of management. Where the utility's management was unusually efficient and economical, a higher rate of return was always allowed. On the other hand, where the management was inefficient and wasteful, a rate of return that would otherwise be regarded as confiscatory was often held to be fair. Various tests were applied to determine the relative efficiency and economy of the management of utility companies. The most common test was a comparison of the prevailing rate schedule with the rate schedules of other companies providing the same service under similar conditions. The Nevada Commission, for example, allowed a return of more than 10 per cent to a water company whose rates were unusually low, and allowed a return of only 3 per cent to another water company whose rates were unusually high. The practice of comparing utility rates—that is, the use of a yardstick—to de-

---

[7] On the relation of risks of various types to the fair rate of return, see *Gates v. Bridgeport Toll Bridge Co.* (Wisc.), P. U. R. 1915 E, 602; *Public Service Commission v. Nevada-California Power Co.* (Nev.), P. U. R. 1915 E, 592; *Re Mountain States Telephone & Telegraph Co.* (Col.), P. U. R. 1917 B, 198.

termine the efficiency and the economy of the management of a public utility enterprise has long been common, and the courts have sustained the legality of giving weight to this factor in determining the fair rate of return.[8]

Consideration has occasionally been given to factors other than those discussed above in determining fair rate of return. Thus, past earnings or losses have been permitted to affect the fair rate of return by some commissions, although the view of the courts has generally been that under ordinary conditions, the record of past earnings does not enter into the determination of the fair rate of return. Again, where the difficulty of raising new capital has been found to be unusually great, some commissions have permitted a relatively high rate of return to be earned, partly as an inducement to new investment, partly as a means of providing for expansion out of surplus. In general, however, the factors given greatest, if not exclusive, consideration in determining the fair rate of return have been the prevailing interest rate, the risks, and the efficiency of the enterprise.

4. The Supreme Court on Value and Return

Public utilities commissions developed their procedure and methods for determining fair value and fair rate of return from the rate making rule laid down in *Smyth v. Ames*. From time to time the Supreme Court has attempted to clarify the rate making rule. In fact, however, the decisions of the court have not been sufficiently definite to permit the development of a uniform rule for determining fair value and the fair rate of return. The inconclusiveness of the court's decisions on the major questions of valuation and return was a necessary consequence of the complexity of the rate making rule. The issues before the court were seldom clearly defined, and they were frequently complicated by a diversity of modifying circumstances that did not permit the application of a uniform rule. Although the decisions

[8] For Nevada, see *Re Fort Scott & Nevada Light, Heat, Water & Power Co.*, P. U. R. 1915 F, 512, and *Public Service Commission v. Carson Water Co.*, P. U. R. 1916 D, 678. See also, *Milwaukee v. Milwaukee Gas Light Co.* (Wisc.), P. U. R. 1920 F, 833; *Mattoon v. Coles County Telephone & Telegraph Co.* (Ill.), P. U. R. 1915 C, 660; *Re Etna Development Co.* (Calif.), P. U. R. 1916 A, 134.

of the Supreme Court did not establish a valuation formula, there was steadily increasing emphasis in its opinions on the importance of reproduction cost less depreciation as an acceptable measure of rate making value.[9] An analysis of the decisions and the opinions of the Supreme Court on valuation from 1898 to 1915 will clarify this distinction.

The cases before the court in this period did not involve the critical valuation question: whether under ordinary circumstances a rate schedule offering a fair rate of return on investment or on reproduction cost, either alone being taken as the measure of fair value, was a denial of the constitutional right of protection to the owners of utility property. In *Smyth v. Ames*, the Supreme Court decided that rates that did not yield a fair return on either reproduction cost or actual cost were confiscatory (169 U. S. 466). In the San Diego cases, 1899 and 1903, the court held that rates that did not yield a fair return on actual cost were not necessarily confiscatory as the investment may have been made under unusual conditions (174 U. S. 739; 189 U. S. 201). In the first Consolidated Gas case, 1909, the court approved a valuation that was in excess of actual cost, so that the sufficiency of rates based on investment was not in question (212 U. S. 19). In the second San Joaquin case, 1914, the court rejected actual cost as the measure of the rate base, but it emphasized the exceptional circumstances in the case (233 U. S. 454). In the Des Moines case, 1915, the court held that reproduction cost under prevailing conditions was not a satisfactory measure of rate making value, but it did not pass on reproduction cost under original conditions (238 U. S. 153). The conclusion from this survey is clearly that the decisions of the Supreme Court from 1898 to 1915 did not establish the predominance of one factor rather than another in the determination of fair value for rate making.

In contrast to these decisions, the dicta of the Supreme Court have tended constantly toward greater emphasis on reproduction cost of the property under original construction conditions. In the first San Diego case, 1899, Justice Harlan said: "What the

[9] This tendency was noted by several writers. See the articles by J. E. Allison and by H. V. Hayes, *Quarterly Journal of Economics*, XXVII, 29 and 616.

company is entitled to demand, in order that it may have just compensation, is a fair return upon the reasonable value of the property at the time it is being used for the public" (154 U. S. 757). The inclusion of the final qualifying phrases is a significant modification of the original statement of the rate making rule. In the second San Diego case, 1903, Justice Holmes cited this statement, and added: "That is decided, and is decided as against the contention that you are to take the actual cost of the plant, annual depreciation, etc., and to allow a fair profit on that footing over the above expenses" (189 U. S. 442). These views were cited in many subsequent valuation cases that came before the Supreme Court as authoritative precedents for the use of reproduction cost as the measure of rate making value.

By the time of the first Consolidated Gas case, 1909, and the Minnesota rate cases, 1913, the dominance of reproduction cost in the expressions of the court on valuation was apparent, and it was strengthened by the opinions in these cases. In the Consolidated Gas case, Justice Peckham said: "The value of the property is to be determined as of the time when the inquiry is made regarding the rates. If the property, which legally enters into the consideration of the question of rates, has increased in value since it was acquired, the company is entitled to the benefit of such increase" (212 U. S. 52). Under exceptional circumstances, the court recognized, a value so determined might not be fair. In the Minnesota rate cases, Justice Hughes stated what had by then clearly become the definite attitude of the court on valuation (230 U. S. 454):

It is clear that in ascertaining the present value we are not limited to the consideration of the amount of the actual investment. If that has been reckless or improvident, losses may be sustained which the community does not underwrite. As the company may not be protected in its actual investment, if the value of the property be plainly less, so the making of a just return for the use of the property involves the recognition of its fair value if it be more than its cost. The property is held in private ownership and it is that property, and not the original cost of it, of which the owner may not be deprived without due process of law.

In the period before the war, public utilities commissions had little difficulty in determining a fair rate of return acceptable to the courts. In the early rate making cases, those before the rate making rule of 1898, the Supreme Court seemed to draw a distinction between a just return and a return that was insufficient but nevertheless not confiscatory. By 1898, when the rate making question was frequently before the court, this view was abandoned. Thereafter, the Supreme Court was inclined to regard the fair rate of return as a compensatory return, the determination of which must be a matter of judgment, subject to the approval of the court. "There is no particular rate of compensation," the court said in the first Consolidated Gas case, "which must in all cases and in all parts of the country be regarded as sufficient for capital invested in business enterprises. Such compensation must depend greatly upon circumstances and locality" (212 U. S. 48). In general, the Supreme Court was disposed to hold that a rate of return commonly regarded as reasonable could not be in violation of the constitutional guaranties on property, except in most unusual cases. In the years before the war, a return of 6 per cent was generally held by the court to be sufficiently compensatory to meet the requirements of the rate making rule.[10]

[10] In the following cases the Supreme Court approved a return of 6 per cent: *Stanislaus County v. San Joaquin & Kings River Canal & Irrigation Co.*, 192 U. S. 201; *Willcox v. Consolidated Gas Co.*, 212 U. S. 19; *Cedar Rapids Gas Co. v. Cedar Rapids*, 223 U. S. 655; *Des Moines Gas Co. v. Des Moines*, 238 U. S. 153.

CHAPTER III

THE PRICE LEVEL, VALUATION, AND RETURN

1. FLUCTUATIONS IN PRICES AND INTEREST RATES

THE UNCERTAINTY surrounding the interpretation of fair value and fair rate of return led to the hope that in time a uniform rule would be developed to eliminate the distractive and expensive litigation in rate making. The failure to develop a uniform rule has led to general condemnation of the rate making principle stated by the Supreme Court in *Smyth v. Ames*.[1] Although much of this criticism has unquestionably been justified, some of it has been extravagant. It is obvious that in 1898, when the rate making rule was laid down, the Supreme Court could not have foreseen the later ramifications of the question, and could not have formulated uniform methods of determining fair value and fair rate of return. The difficulties at that time were insuperable. Utility accounting was unregulated, and satisfactory records of cost and investment were not available. Valuation was of necessity a matter of judgment. Nor could a uniform method of determining fair rate of return be established for all utilities. Some were pioneers in new and speculative industries; others came into fields already well developed in which risks were at a minimum. Many utilities, particularly railroads, were established prior to the policy of regulation; and no utility enprise was undertaken in contemplation of any particular method of determining fair return.

Even today the economic aspects of rate making are so complex that a uniform rule on valuation and return must be developed with great care. A uniform rule would have to be applied to such diverse industries as railroads, street railways, gas, electricity, telephone and telegraphs, water supply, and the nu-

---

[1] See, for example, the articles by Dean Goddard, *Michigan Law Review*, XXII, 652, 777, the article by Judge Hand, *Michigan Law Review*, XXIV, 466, and the dissenting opinion of Justice Brandeis in *Southwestern Bell Telephone Co. v. Public Service Commission of Missouri*, 262 U. S. 276.

merous minor utility industries. These industries are confronted with different economic problems. For some, the future will bring a need for tremendous expansion, for others there is the prospect of gradual decline. The demand for the services of some utilities is elastic, for others inelastic. Some utility services enter into further production, others do not. These are obvious differences. The wisdom of indiscriminately applying to such diverse utilities a uniform rule on valuation and return, developed and applied after the companies have been operating for some time, may be doubted.

Although the legal and economic difficulties have been a great obstacle to the development of a uniform rule, the principal obstacle has unquestionably been the great fluctuations in prices and interest rates. With a stable price level, the two fundamental methods of valuation—prudent investment and reproduction cost—tend to be the same. There is then no great financial advantage to consumers or producers of utility services in either method of valuation, and there would probably be no objection to the gradual development of a uniform method of valuation. Similarly, with stable interest rates, the fair rate of return would be subject to little variation. With rising and falling prices and interest rates, however, fair value and fair rate of return show such large and important movements that companies and consumers have a great interest in establishing their views on rate making. The litigation in rate making cases has varied with the size of the financial stake—that is, with the magnitude of fluctuations in prices and interest rates. The tremendous rise in prices and interest rates from 1915 to 1920 intensified the eagerness of utility companies and consumers to have their methods of rate making adopted. With the rapid decline in prices and interest rates from 1929 to 1933, the situation has changed somewhat. It may be that the financial interests of utility producers and consumers are now so nearly balanced with different methods of rate making that an acceptable uniform rule may be developed.

The manner in which a rise or fall in the price level affects producers and consumers of utility services is obvious. With a rise in prices, the operating expenses of utility companies are increased, and their net return at given schedules of rates is decreased. The return being insufficient, the utilities demand new schedules with a higher level of rates. The process of revising rates must involve, under the due process clause as interpreted by the courts, a new fair value and a new fair rate of return. In the new valuation consideration must be given to reproduction cost, which increases with the rise in prices. A higher rate base must therefore be established. Similarly, the rise in prices will have been accompanied by higher interest rates, and a higher fair rate of return will have to be allowed. On the other hand, with a fall in prices, consumers will object to the maintenance of prevailing rate schedules, particularly as their incomes will have declined. The lower operating expenses, and the decreased reproduction cost and rate of return, will require a downward revision of utility rates.

These rate making problems are always before commissions, for even moderate movements of the price level are accompanied by requests for rate revision. But when the change in prices is large and rapid, the necessity of revising rates, fair value, and fair rate of return under the complex rate making procedure required by law imposes a heavy burden upon utilities commissions. It is just at such times that the need is most urgent for a uniform rule for determining fair value and fair rate of return by methods not involving great expense or delay. A consideration of the feasibility and desirability of establishing a uniform rule requires an understanding of the relative merits of the different methods of determining fair value and fair rate of return.

2. VALUATION AT CURRENT REPRODUCTION COST

In this brief discussion of the economic aspects of reproduction cost, prudent investment, and fair rate of return, the constitutional question will not be considered. It is not the purpose of this study to determine whether the Supreme Court's interpretation of fair value and of fair return is legally sound. No consideration, therefore, is given to the legal theories that the taking of utility property is done once for all at the time the original investment is made—thus justifying the use of prudent investment; or that the taking of utility property for public use is a process continuous with the provision of utility services— thus justifying the use of reproduction cost. Probably either interpretation is legally sound, provided it is the intention of the legislature and of utility investors to regard one or another of these views as determinant in its regulation and in their investment. The purpose of this study is to determine which of the methods of measuring fair value and fair rate of return is economically most desirable, and to consider the best means for establishing the uniform use of the most desirable rate making method.

It is generally argued by those favoring the use of reproduction cost as the measure of rate making value, that in a society of free enterprise this method of determining fair value is likely to bring about the most desirable volume of production of utility services. Under free enterprise, the proportion of the productive resources of the community engaged in supplying goods and services of various kinds is determined by the community's demand for these commodities at prevailing costs of production. In a period of changing demand, it is recognized that for a time the quantities of some goods and services produced may be more or less than this economically desirable amount, for where productive equipment is durable it is difficult to diminish the amount of production, and where productive equipment has a long period of gestation it is difficult to increase the amount of production, in short periods. Nevertheless, the desirable amount of productive effort engaged in supplying the various goods and services tends to be the amount that will produce the quantity of commodities that can be sold at approximately prevailing costs of production.

If the fair value for rate making is determined on any other basis than the current reproduction cost of the utility's property, the price of utility services to the public must be somewhat more or less than the prevailing cost of producing these services. It must then follow that if rates are too low, an undesirably large amount of the labor and capital of the community will be engaged in providing utility services—and some of the labor and capital producing utility services would be more useful economically if they were devoted to other production. On the other hand, if rates are too high, an undesirably small amount of the labor and capital of the community will be engaged in providing utility services—and some of the labor and capital producing other commodities would be more useful if they were devoted to the production of utility services. Only the use of reproduction cost as the rate base, it is argued, can bring about the proper division of the productive resources of the community between industries providing utility services and industries providing other goods and services.

There can be little doubt of the fundamental soundness of this view. It is necessary to observe, however, that in practice the use of reproduction cost as the rate base does not succeed in fixing utility rates at the prevailing cost of producing these services. The reason for this is clear when the method used in determining reproduction cost is considered. Reproduction cost in the economic sense means the current cost of constructing utility plants using the equipment and methods of production of a representative firm. Thus, if larger units or different types of equipment have become more economical, it is the cost of producing utility services with larger units of the newer equipment that is the economically ideal rate for utility services. Reproduction cost, so interpreted, means the cost of constructing a representative modern plant capable of providing equivalent services. In fact, however, the Supreme Court has held that in valuing utility property reproduction cost must be defined as the present cost of constructing the existing plant under original conditions. Under the circumstances, reproduction cost is very unlikely to be the proper basis for rate making, particularly in those utility industries in which rapid technical progress has been made.[2]

Two other points, indicating that reproduction cost is not the ideal rate base, are worth noting. The reproduction cost

[2] For a more extended consideration of this point, see J. Bauer and N. Gold, *Public Utility Valuation for Purposes of Rate Control,* Chap. VI. See also, Chap. X, section 2 below.

under present valuation procedure is determined by estimates that cannot, in fact, be tested in actual construction. Strikingly large differences are commonly found in reproduction cost estimates made by engineering experts for commissions and for utility companies. It should also be noted that under present valuation procedure many months, occasionally years, may elapse between the time the valuation is made and the time the new rates are put into effect. Consequently, even at best, the use of reproduction cost as the rate base does not result in establishing rates equal to the current cost of producing utility services, but rates equal to the approximate cost of production at some more or less recent time in the past. It is useless to attempt to secure through a rate base determined by reproduction cost as defined by the courts, a precise duplication of the forces that regulate prices in competitive industry.

It is sometimes argued that reproduction cost is the most desirable basis for determining fair return from the point of view of the investor. A change in the value of money will manifest itself in a change in the current cost of constructing utility property. A fair return on a rate base determined by reproduction cost may be a variable money return, but in terms of purchasing power, it is said, the return is likely to show a great degree of stability. As between a stable return in money or in purchasing power, there can be no question that greater justice is attained through the latter. It must be emphasized, however, that a rate base determined by reproduction cost does not give a stable income in purchasing power to each class of utility investor. The larger part of the investment in utility companies is in the form of fixed income securities—bonds and preferred stock. The use of reproduction cost as the rate base would not alter the money income of such investors with changing prices, and would not assure them a stable return in purchasing power. On the other hand, the use of reproduction cost would tend to give the owners of common stock an extremely large return in purchasing power during periods of rising prices, and an extremely small return in purchasing power during periods of falling prices. The use of reproduction cost cannot assure investors a more stable real income from their investment in utility enterprises.

Whatever the supposed advantages of the use of reproduction cost in valuation may be from the economic point of view, there can be little question that from the administrative point of view, its use necessitates an undesirably complex valuation procedure, costly in time and in money. Further, the differences in estimates of reproduction cost, even when made by disinterested experts, are so large that litigation is encouraged. These administrative difficulties are the fundamental objections to the use of reproduction cost as the rate base.

3. Valuation at Prudent Investment

The great advantages of prudent investment valuation are all related to the ease with which the rate base may be determined by this method of valuation. When once the prudent investment in a utility enterprise is established, the fair value at any given time may be determined from the accounting records: to the original cost is added the cost of additions and betterments, and from this is deducted the cost of property retired and the reserves allowed for depreciation. In contrast to the ease of determining fair value in this manner are the difficulties of valuation by the reproduction cost method: the preparation of a detailed inventory, the determination of fair unit prices, the conflicting opinions of experts for companies and for consumers, and the prospect that differences that cannot be settled must be taken to the courts. All of this procedure is expensive, and prevents the prompt and proper adjustment of rates to changing conditions of cost.

Even from the economic point of view there are advantages so great as to justify a preference for prudent investment rather than reproduction cost valuation. If operating expenses have risen, and with them reproduction cost, the determination of new rates under the present valuation procedure requires an entirely new valuation. When many utility companies request rate revisions, years may elapse before new valuations can be completed. In the meantime, it is conceivable that actual rates will remain below the level that would be promptly fixed if fair value were measured by prudent investment. Similarly, a decline in operating expenses, and with it probably in reproduction cost also, cannot result in an immediate revision of rates. Thus, with reproduction cost valuation the community does not have the correspondence of rates and costs that is commonly assumed. In fact, the use of reproduction cost necesitates considerable rigidity of rates because of the time required for valuation. Rate making by the prudent investment method would bring about a more prompt, although perhaps not so complete, adjustment of rates to costs. It may therefore be argued that even from the economic point of view prudent investment is the superior basis for valuation.

Another factor to be considered is that the present rate making procedure is unusually expensive, largely because of the importance of the reproduction cost method of valuation. This expense is part of the cost of providing utility services to the community. It may be said with justification that in the long run the total cost of producing utility services would be less with the use of prudent investment valuation than with the use of the reproduction cost method. This lowered cost may be more than sufficient to offset whatever remains of the theoretical advantage there may be in the reproduction cost method of valuation. The expense of valuing utilities in this country in the period of rapidly changing prices, 1916 to 1936, has been in the hundreds of millions of dollars. This is an economy in the use of the prudent investment method of valuation that cannot be overlooked.

There is one other question that must be considered: whether the use of prudent investment valuation will permit the continued flow of funds necessary for the expansion of the utility industries. As has already been indicated, the greater part of the investment in utility enterprises has been by holders of fixed income securities. For such investors prudent investment would be the more desirable rate base. A sufficiently large fall in the reproduction cost of utility property could imperil the basis for the earnings necessary to meet the contractual obligations to such investors. Prudent investment as the rate base would add further assurance to the relative certainty of their income. It is probable that with prudent investment valuation, the provision of capital for utility undertakings through bonds and preferred stock could be made at lower interest and dividend costs than now. As for holders of common stock, it is possible that their purchase of such securities indicates a preference for a variable money income with greater stability in the purchasing power of that income. In fact, there is little stability in the purchasing power of the income of common stockholders in utility companies. By necessity they become speculators on the prospective movement of prices. A rise in prices means that as beneficiaries of a higher rate base they gain in real income as well as in money income; and with a fall in prices they lose in real income as well as in money income.

Two important motives for investment in common stock may be recognized. First, some purchasers of common stocks feel that the larger return is more than compensatory for the additional risk. It is probable that the average return on common stocks is sufficiently larger than the average return on bonds and preferred stocks to offset the greater risk. Second, some purchasers of common stocks are willing and eager to take the risks of price and interest movements in the hope of profiting from a fortuitous rise in prices and in interest rates. The stockholders who invest in common stocks because of the larger net return may not all be desirous of assuming the risks of price and interest changes. Such stockholders would be benefited by a prudent investment rate base. Few investors in utility securities, it seems, would be adversely affected by prudent investment valuation. There is reason to believe, therefore, that capital for the utility industries could be raised at less cost, on the whole, with prudent investment than with reproduction cost valuation.

4. CAPITAL COST AND RATE OF RETURN

In discussions of rate making, less emphasis has been given to the problem of determining fair rate of return than to the problem of valuation. In fact, the fair rate of return has never been a matter of major controversy except in periods of rapidly changing interest rates. There are two reasons why little controversy has developed on the question of the rate of return. First, fair rate of return is less variable than is fair value measured by the reproduction cost method. Thus, in the period since 1900, the lowest rate of return that has generally been approved as fair was 6 per cent. In the periods of rapidly rising interest rates, during the war and again in the late 1920's, a rate of return of 8 or 9 per cent was generally regarded as the maximum necessary for a compensatory return. The difference between these highest and lowest fair rates of return is large, but it is not as large as the highest and lowest construction cost levels in the same period. A second reason why the rate of return is a less controversial problem in rate making is that its determination is free from complex and expensive procedure. Although there are differences of opinion as to what may be a fair rate of return, there is no attempt to prove the fairness of one rate rather than another in the elaborate and costly manner in which fair value is proved.

The most important factor in determining the fair rate of return is the prevailing interest rate. The tendency for the interest rate to remain relatively stable has been noted by many writers; but this assumed stability is a long run normal phenomenon. In periods of social, political, or economic disturbance, there may be considerable variation in interest rates. Large fluctuations in interest rates are generally associated with war and with extreme changes in business conditions. Obviously, wartime is a period of great demand for loanable funds. The great destruction and consumption of war goods necessitates government borrowing and price inflation, both of which affect interest rates. The rise in interest rates in wartime is generally followed by a slow decline in the postwar period. Similarly, a period of great prosperity is accompanied by a rise in interest rates, and a period of great depression by a fall in interest rates. For these reasons the fair rate of return on utility property, as determined by courts and commissions, fluctuated considerably from 1916 to 1936.

The return paid to bondholders and to preferred stockholders is fixed by the terms of their contracts; and any variation in the fair rate of return generally affects only the common stockholders. In a period of rising interest rates, common stockholders gain an unexpectedly larger return. On the other hand, in a period of falling interest rates, the return to bondholders and to preferred stockholders must be maintained. The loss then falls entirely on the common stockholders. Because the variability of the fair rate of return introduces an element of uncertainty in the earnings of utility companies, it is probable that the interest rate on utility bonds, and the dividend rate on utility preferred stocks must be somewhat higher than they would otherwise be. Nor are common stockholders always desirous of assuming the risks of variable utility earnings. Their fortuitous gains and losses with fluctuations in the interest rate serve no useful purpose, and may add to the cost of securing utility capital through the issue of common stock.

Apart from the possible increased cost of raising utility capital, there is another objection that is occasionally raised to the present method of determining fair rate of return. Under the present method, consideration is given to the prevailing interest rate, the risks of the business, and the efficiency of the management. No consideration is given to the manner in which the capital is raised—whether in the form of bonds, preferred stock, or common stock. Thus, if a fair rate of return of 6 per cent or 8 per cent is allowed to a utility company, this rate of return is not affected by the fact that the company may have an unusually large part of its capital provided through bonds and preferred stock. Indirectly, of course, this factor may enter into the determination of the fair rate of return. A utility company whose business is regarded as being unusually free from risk may be allowed a lower rate of return; and it is precisely such companies with more stable earning power that ordinarily raise much of their capital by the issue of bonds and preferred stock.

Neglect of the capital structure of a utility company in determining the fair rate of return may result in giving to common stockholders an unusually high return. Thus, assuming that a utility company raises 60 per cent of its capital from the issue of bonds and preferred stock on which the average return is 6 per cent, and assuming that the fair rate of return allowed on the fair value of the property—say, actual investment—is 8 per cent, then the return to the common stockholders of this utility company will be 11 per cent. The larger the proportion of securities bearing a fixed return, and the greater the difference between the fair rate of return and the average return to preferred security holders, the larger will be the net return to common stockholders. It cannot be doubted that this method of applying the rate of return to the value of the property may, under certain conditions, yield an unfairly high rate of return to common stockholders at the expense of the consumers of utility services.

In competitive business, the return that is earned by a company is not independent of the manner in which the business may be financed. Thus, if certain industries, because of greater stability of earnings, are able to raise a large part of their capital through issues of low rate fixed income securities, the return to the common stockholders will not for this reason become unusually large. The tendency in competitive industry must be toward equality of return to common stockholders, allowance being made for differences in risk. Under normal conditions, prices in competitive industry are sufficient to meet operating expenses and capital charges, provided capital is raised in the economical manner available to a representative firm. By analogy, the fair return for public utilities should be determined by allowing the fixed and contingent charges—say, as capital operating expenses—and then determining the fair rate of return on the basis of the common stockholders' interest in the utility property. Thus, a return of 8 per cent would mean 8 per cent on the common stockholders' share rather than on the total fair value of the utility property.

These perplexing problems of valuation and return are unavoidable if the present rate making procedure is continued, and if methods of production, prices, and interest rates continue to change. So difficult are these problems in periods of rapid change that it becomes impossible, from an administrative point of view, to make efficient use of the present rate making procedure. Partly for this reason special methods of determining fair value and fair rate of return were devised and used in the abnormal war and postwar periods. It is significant that these war and postwar methods of determining value and return offer a suggestion for a way out of our present rate making difficulties.

CHAPTER IV

WARTIME REGULATION AND RATE MAKING

1. The Objects of Wartime Rate Making

The OUTSTANDING feature of the wartime regulation of public utilities is the extensive control exercised by state and federal authorities. Under the pressure of war needs, the federal government undertook the operation of railroads and telephones, and through its numerous war boards it exercised considerable indirect control. In nearly all states, the regulatory powers of utilities commissions were extended by laws granting them extraordinary emergency authority. Even more important was the extension of commission authority with the implied consent of the courts and the utility companies. The greater federal control during the war was distinctly helpful to state commissions. It relieved them of the burden of regulation and rate making for an important group of utilities at a time when commissions were hard pressed for facilities to carry on their work. Further, the increase in railroad and telephone rates under federal operation was a useful precedent for granting to local utilities the higher rates essential for the maintenance of service.

Public utilities commissions had two objects in wartime rate making: to maintain uninterrupted service, and to minimize the rise in utility rates. With the rapidly rising price level of 1915 to 1920, these objects could not have been attained if commissions had not been permitted to determine rates without the use of the established rate making procedure. The magnitude of the increase in operating expenses between 1915 and 1920 is indicated by the 100 per cent rise in union rates of hourly wages, and the 170 per cent rise in the price of bituminous coal. With such a large and rapid increase in operating expenses, few utility companies could maintain service with the revenues derived from the prewar rate schedules. To secure a fair return on the value of their property, whether determined on the basis of investment or reproduction cost, was out of the question for many utility companies. The immediate need was to increase revenues sufficiently to meet the higher operating expenses.

It is difficult to overestimate the importance that the federal government attached to the maintenance of local utility service during the war. A breakdown in the operation of street railways, gas, and electric power plants would have restricted production in essential war industries. To maximize war efforts, these utility services had to be maintained by assuring to utility companies rates sufficient to meet the costs of operation and other necessary expenses. In a letter to President Wilson in February, 1918, when operating expenses had risen to a very high level, Secretary McAdoo emphasized the danger of a general suspension of production in the utility industries unless state commissions took action to remedy the situation. He called for a sympathetic attitude toward the needs of utility companies in the period of high prices. So important was the maintenance of local utility service for successful operation of the war that a general breakdown of production under local regulation would inevitably have led to some form of federal control of local utilities for the duration of the war.[1]

Despite the urgent recommendations of the federal authorities, many commissions were disinclined to raise utility rates, particularly to the level necessary to yield a fair return on the fair value of the property. With the continued rise in prices in the early postwar period, the situation became even more serious. In March, 1919, the President called a conference of Governors and Mayors to meet at the White House to discuss, among other questions, the plight of the public utility companies. The utility executives presented a strong plea for increased rates, but the conference made no immediate recommendations. The situation had become so serious, particularly for street railways, that the President appointed the National Electric Railway Commission "to investigate, study, and report upon the general problem and status of the electric railway industry of America generally, without taking up any local situation, in order that state and

[1] For the letter of Secretary McAdoo and the reply of President Wilson, see P. U. R. 1918 D, 223-25.

municipal authorities may have the benefit of full information and of any conclusions reached."[2] The difficulties were not, in fact, confined to the street railways. The proceedings of the various utility associations from 1917 to 1923 show that the rapid rise in expenses and the lagging change in utility rates presented a difficult problem to utility companies in this period.

2. THE DOCTRINE OF CORPORATE NEEDS

Rate making procedure before the war was designed to provide careful and deliberate consideration of the legal rights of a utility company that was operating under an inadequate rate structure. Rarely were rates so low as to provide less revenue than the operating expenses. There was, therefore, no great danger of suspension of service, and a utility company could await a careful investigation of its needs, with a view to determining a schedule of rates that would yield a fair rate of return on the fair value of its property. Inadequate rates were a particular, not a general, condition. Commissions could undertake a rate case in the deliberate manner that had been developed to meet the constitutional requirement of due process. Under war conditions, with the need for frequent general revision of rates, commissions could not use the ordinary procedure without risking a suspension of service during the long period required for rate making. It was clearly impossible for commissions to undertake new valuations and to determine new fair rates of return whenever higher rates were necessary. A change in rate making procedure was essential.

Even under normal conditions rate making was a slow and expensive process. If the company was small and of local importance, the fair value and the fair rate of return could be determined within a few weeks at a cost of 1 or 2 per cent of the rate base. If the company was large and served a wide area, the rate proceedings might last for two or three years, and the cost

[2] For reports of the conference, see *The New York Times*, February 26 to March 6, 1919. For reports of the Commission's hearings, and for other utility investigations at this time, see *The New York Times*, May 21, 22, 30, June 6, August 15, September 15 to 19, and September 30, 1919.

to all parties might be more than 4 per cent of the rate base.[3]
To adjust rates promptly in this period of rapidly rising prices,
commissions frequently dispensed with the determination of a
new fair value. The situation was aptly summarized by the
Missouri Commission. In refusing a request for a new valuation in a rate case, the commission said:

As much as the Commission desires to have before it a complete
inventory and appraisement of a public utility before reaching a conclusion as to a reasonable rate to cover the service rendered, it has
found it wholly impractical in many instances during these extraordinary times in the world's history to demand it as a condition
precedent. The Commission is not unmindful of the fact, with labor
and fuel prices ascending skyward by leaps and bounds, that during
the interim of time that the expert doctors are making a diagnosis
by a long, laborious inventory and appraisal of the public service
utilities of our state, the patient would very likely succumb, and the
resultant thereof be that the public would be without service.[4]

The necessary simplicity and elasticity in rate making procedure were provided by emergency rate making laws. Under
these, commissions were authorized to fix new rates without
the formality of the customary procedure. The existence of
an emergency was established by proof that revenues under rate
schedules in force were insufficient to meet operating expenses.
Under such conditions new rates could be fixed on the basis
of a temporary or *prima facie* rate making value without reference to the fair value of the utility's property as usually determined. To hasten the revision of rates, commissions frequently
granted a horizontal increase, and to assure the adequacy of the
rate schedule for some time, provision was occasionally made
for a sliding scale of surcharges—the familiar fuel price device.
Such rates were necessarily makeshift, and in some instances
they were probably unfair and oppressive. However, they accomplished their primary purpose: to adjust rates promptly and

---

[3] The length of time required for valuation and rate making in Pennsylvania
averaged two and a half years in nineteen important rate cases. See M. L. Cooke,
Public Utility Regulation, p. 235.

[4] *Re City Light & Traction Co.* (Mo.), P. U. R. 1918 F, 938.

to assure continued service in a period of rapidly rising operating expenses.[5]

In neglecting to determine rates that would yield a fair rate of return on the fair value of the utility property, commissions in reality abandoned the long established rate making rule. The new emergency rule, it may be said, was that rates should be at least sufficient to meet the corporate needs essential to the maintenance of service. The origin of the principle that corporate needs must be the basis for emergency rate making is obscure. In his letter to President Wilson, Secretary McAdoo said that "united effort will be necessary to meet alike the public requirements for service, and the corporate financial needs upon which that service depends." Even before the war, however, some state laws provided that rates must be at least sufficient to meet the obligations of the utility company under its security issues. The Maryland Public Service Commission Law of 1910, for example, stated that every rate making "valuation shall be so made and ascertained by the Commission that as far as possible it shall not disturb the value of bonds of any of said corporations issued prior to the passage of this act."[6] It is possible that in providing that consideration be given to the par and market value of the bonds and stocks of the utility company in valuation, something similar to the doctrine of corporate financial needs may have been implied by the Supreme Court in the case of *Smyth v. Ames*.

The great usefulness of the rule of corporate financial needs for emergency rate making is apparent. Its general application, even during the difficult rate making period of the war, was nevertheless impossible. Although the courts were tolerant in permitting commissions to fix utility rates at a level much below that required under the rate making rule, they never entirely abandoned the principle that rates must yield a fair rate of return on a fair value of the utility property.

[5] For an extended note on devices for adjusting rates, see P. U. R. 1919 C, 876.

[6] Section 30 of the Law of 1910. Cited by the Maryland Commission, *Re United Railways & Electric Co. of Baltimore*, P. U. R. 1919 C, 74, 85, and held to be mandatory, P. U. R. 1920 A, 1. The doctrine of corporate needs is further discussed in Chap. VIII, section 4, below.

It is interesting to note the relation of the doctrine of corporate needs to the prudent investment method of determining fair value and to the common stock basis for return. In normal times, rates based on corporate needs would yield revenue sufficient to meet operating expenses, including depreciation, the interest on bonded debt, the required dividends on preferred stock, and the normal dividends on common stock. If the issue of securities were controlled by the commission, as it generally is, the rate base would then be equivalent to prudent investment, and the fair return would be determined by the capital charges required to meet the obligations incurred through the issue of the securities. It should be added that in fixing rates on the basis of corporate needs, commissions did not always regard normal dividends on common stock as part of the essential corporate financial needs in the war period.

3. UTILITY RATES AND THE BURDENS OF WAR

One of the primary objects of wartime rate making was to avoid, so far as possible, the large increase that would be necessary if utility rates were fixed to yield a fair rate of return on the fair value of the utility property as these would be determined by the usual rate making procedure. By interpreting fair rate of return and fair value to mean normal rate of return and normal value, commissions avoided giving effect to the higher wartime interest rates and the higher wartime construction costs. To justify the use of normal rate of return and normal value, commissions laid great emphasis on the unusual conditions that prevailed during the war, and on the supreme importance of the public welfare in determining the proper level of utility rates at such a time.

In establishing this policy of maintaining rates at a level below that necessary to yield a fair rate of return on the reproduction cost of utility property, commissions relied for authority on Justice Peckham's opinion in the first Consolidated Gas case. Although in this case the court said that "if the property, which legally enters into the consideration of the question of rates, has increased in value since it was acquired, the company is entitled to the benefit of such increase," a specific exception was made "where the property may have increased so enormously in value as to render a rate permitting a return upon such increased value unjust to the public" (212 U. S. 52). To many commissions, the special circumstances of war seemed reason enough for invoking the exception that Justice Peckham recognized to reproduction cost valuation.

At one time or another nearly every state commission announced that it would not allow the higher interest rates and construction costs of the war period to become the basis for utility rates. "There is no foundation in equity, justice or law," said the Missouri Commission, "for using abnormally high current prices . . . in fixing value for rate making purposes" (P. U. R. 1919 E, 211). The Nebraska Commission said: "If conditions promised to make such prices permanent there might be good reason for using them as a basis for valuation figures, but it is universally conceded that present conditions are abnormal and may terminate at any time" (P. U. R. 1917 E, 475). The Washington Department of Public Works said that it neither considered nor allowed current prices to affect its valuations in the period of high prices (P. U. R. 1921 D, 765). To comply with the rate making rule, these commissions fixed rates that yielded a normal rate of return on the normal value of the utility property.

Commissions gave great emphasis to war factors as a justification for low utility rates. It was commonly charged by consumers' organizations that in seeking a rate structure based on wartime prices and interest rates, utility companies were attempting to profiteer. Even Chief Justice Hughes, then acting as referee for the New York Supreme Court, held in his report in the Brooklyn Borough Gas case that to allow rates to be based on abnormally high current reproduction costs would be to permit a public utility company to profit from a public disaster. He said: "To base rates upon a plant valuation simply representing a hypothetical cost of reproduction at a time of abnormally high price due to exceptional conditions . . . would result in allowing a public service corporation to take advantage of a public calamity by increasing its rates above what would be a liberal return not only on actual investment, but upon a normal reproduction cost" (P. U. R. 1918 F, 347-348).

Even greater stress was laid on the great sacrifices the country was making to carry on the war as a justification for requiring public utility companies to share in these sacrifices by accepting somewhat less than their normal return. "The war's burden in the form of taxes," said the Arizona Commission, "has been laid heavily upon the entire population, and we are of the opinion that the public utility companies should be content with something considerably less than their normal return" (P. U. R. 1919 C, 877). The Minnesota Commission did not go quite so far, but it held that "corporations as well as individuals must bear their share of the burdens of war and must sustain some loss of income without flinching" (P. U. R. 1919 C, 877). A conciliatory view of the position of utility companies in this abnormal period was taken by the Connecticut Commission. In the Hartford Street Railway case, the commission said: "The natural result of war conditions is to add burdens, but these burdens should as far as possible be equitably distributed. . . . That which in normal times would be a fair return in the way of dividends for capital invested might in wartime cause an unequal distribution of the burdens in favor of the stockholders" (P. U. R. 1918 C, 611).

This attitude toward utility rates and utility earnings was in many instances carried to undesirable extremes. The California Railroad Commission prided itself that while during the war and the early postwar period prices had advanced as much as 72 to 300 per cent, the average advance in utility rates in California did not exceed 40 per cent. "The utilities were not permitted to earn a larger percentage upon the value of their property than in the prewar period. The Commission did not allow them to earn unusual or unreasonable profits, even despite the fact that money invested during the period in almost every other form of security or enterprise earned higher returns than it had before."[7] How far the earnings of utility companies might

[7] H. W. Brundige, *Regulation of Public Utilities*, California Railroad Commission, Report for 1922.

have been reduced under the theory of sharing the burdens of war it is difficult to say. The movement in this direction was checked by the decision of the Federal District Court in the Toledo street railway case, 1919, that a utility could not be required to operate at a loss on the ground that it ought to share the burdens of war.[8]

4. Wartime Methods of Valuation

During and immediately after the war, commissions used various valuation methods for the purpose of maintaining rate making values of public utility property below reproduction cost at current unit prices. Each of these methods was ostensibly in compliance with the valuation principles of *Smyth v. Ames* as originally laid down in 1898 and developed by the courts since then. Despite the explicit statement of the factors affecting fair value in the rate making rule, commissions found little difficulty in applying methods appropriate for maintaining low valuations. It is important to note that for a time some of these wartime methods of valuation were approved by the courts as conforming to the requirements of the rate making rule.

Wartime valuation methods may be conveniently classified in three groups. The first gave great weight to the extraordinary war conditions and admittedly departed from accepted methods of valuation. The valuations of this type were of a tentative nature, resembling in many respects the emergency valuations discussed above. The second group gave consideration to all the factors required by the rate making rule, but gave little or no weight to reproduction cost in the final rate base. The third group gave consideration to all factors, and also gave weight to reproduction cost, although not the dominant weight that had been given to this factor in prewar valuations. This was by far the most important group of valuations. They took into account the requirements of the rate making rule, but modified the earlier interpretation to permit the fixing of rate making values much below the reproduction cost at current unit prices.

[8] *H. L. Doherty & Co. v. Toledo Railways & Light Co.*, P. U. R. 1919 C, 230.

The use of tentative, *prima facie,* approximate, and mini-mum valuations was a device that aided in the prompt deter-mination of rate making value and avoided the expensive pre-war procedure. In the Georgia Railway & Power case, 1918, the commission did not attempt to determine a definite rate base, but found a minimum valuation which was considered satisfac-tory for the purpose of passing on the pending application for higher rates (P. U. R. 1918 F, 624). These informal methods of valuation, in which tentative rate bases were fixed, were an early stage in the development of the more formal wartime methods of valuation. Tentative and approximate valuations were seldom made after 1919. It is questionable whether the courts would have permitted commissions to use such valuation methods after the war had ended.

The valuations based on some form of investment retained the simplicity of these informal valuations and had the added merit of determining one of the factors requiring consideration under the rate making rule. In general, in this group of val-uation methods some consideration was also given to repro-duction cost, but the rate base was fixed at approximately the investment cost.[9] Because it was an effective means of main-taining low valuations, investment cost in its various forms—capitalization, book cost, historical cost—was extensively used. These were not, however, essentially wartime methods of valua-tion. The various measures of investment cost were revived rather than developed to meet war conditions. Ordinarily valua-tion at investment cost had not been regarded as conforming to the principles of *Smyth v. Ames,* and for this reason was of limited usefulness. When utilities undertook to litigate such valuations, the courts invariably sustained the contention that investment cost valuation was a denial of the constitutional rights of owners of utility property.

The third group of wartime valuation methods was definitely developed for the purpose of maintaining low valuations while

[9] See, for example, *Kansas City Railway Co. v. Kansas City* (Mo.), P. U. R. 1918 E, 190; *Re Missouri & Kansas Telephone Co.* (Kans.), P. U. R. 1918 C, 777; *Re Western Colorado Power Co.,* P. U. R. 1918 E, 629.

conforming to a liberal interpretation of the rate making rule. These valuation methods were used in the most important cases, and for a time they had the approval of the courts.[10] Further, they offered a new basis for a permanent valuation policy in which reproduction cost at current unit prices would be given little weight, and in which the expensive and dilatory prewar valuation procedure would be modified. Recently there has been revived discussion of the possibility of adapting these methods of valuation to present needs. For these reasons, the principal wartime methods of valuation—reproduction cost at average unit prices, the use of corrective indices with basic valuations, and the split inventory—merit extended consideration.

[10] See the analysis of wartime valuations in Justice Brandeis's opinion in the Southwestern Bell Telephone case, 262 U. S. 276, 301-2, note 14.

CHAPTER V

VALUATION: REPRODUCTION COST AT AVERAGE UNIT PRICES

I. The Prewar Use of Average Prices

THE RATE MAKING rule required that in determining the fair value of a utility's property, consideration be given to the present as compared with the original cost of construction—that is, reproduction cost. In the valuation procedure developed before the war, reproduction cost was found by applying unit prices to an inventory of the utility's property. These unit prices were based on current prices of labor and materials, on average prices for a period of years before the valuation, or on predicted prices for a future period following the valuation. Prior to the war, current prices were most commonly used. During the war, and for a time after the war, average prices were frequently used in place of current prices in reproduction cost estimates. Whether current prices or average prices were used, the intention was to find the reproduction cost of the property. It was recognized, however, that reproduction cost was not necessarily equivalent to rate making value.

Average unit prices were most commonly used before the war in railroad valuation. Professor Cooley in appraising railroads for the Michigan Board of Tax Commissioners, in 1900, used unit prices which represented the fair average cost during the five-year period preceding the appraisal. The Wisconsin railroad valuation for rate making, in 1903, was on the basis of average prices for five and ten preceding years.[1] When the Valuation Act of 1913 was passed, the railroads submitted a brief asking that in the determination of unit prices, consideration be given to "actual prices (weighted average) and conditions affecting labor and material markets during a period of ten years preceding June 30, 1914, with appropriate consideration to the

[1] *Transactions of the American Society of Civil Engineers*, LXXII, 43, 75.

existence or non-existence of actual railroad construction in that period." In the valuations made by the Interstate Commerce Commission, the value as of a given date was found by applying average unit prices for five and ten years preceding 1914.[2]

There was some use of average unit prices in the valuation of local utilities by state commissions before the war. The practice of the Wisconsin Commission was to take "the reproduction cost new of each item, . . . always guarding against extreme fluctuations in market prices by adopting a five-year average basis for prices wherever practicable" (4 Wisc. R. C. R., 509). The Pennsylvania Public Service Companies Law of 1913 provided that in ascertaining and determining fair value, the commission must consider the reproduction cost of the property based upon the fair average prices of material and labor (P. U. R. 1927 C, 427). The North Dakota law contained a similar provision: "In valuing the property on the basis of the cost to reproduce the same, unit prices of material and labor entering into construction shall be based on the average prices of a sufficient period of years to secure normal results" (P. U. R. 1921 E, 720).

Although the use of average unit prices was not the prevailing method of determining reproduction cost before the war, it was an established and well-recognized method of valuation, and in many states it was held to be preferable to the use of current unit prices. The object in using average unit prices was to avoid the determination of unusually high or low rate making values, as might conceivably result from the use of current prices at the peak of prosperity or in the trough of depression. The period for which average prices were taken varied. In the valuation of railroads the period was comparatively long, five to ten years, in the valuation of local utilities the period was much shorter, two to five years. A distinction must also be made between valuation at average unit prices before the war, and such valuation during and after the war. Before the war the purpose was to eliminate cyclical influences on rate making value while avoiding any bias in favor of high or low valuations. After 1917,

---

[2] *Valuation Brief of 1915,* p. 141. For a fuller discussion of the valuation method of the Interstate Commerce Commission, see Chap. VII, section 4, below.

however, commissions used average prices for the purpose of eliminating the effect of prevailing high prices on valuations.

2. FIVE-YEAR AVERAGE PRICES

When the great rise in the price level became apparent in 1917, many commissions that had used reproduction cost as the measure of rate making value sought some way of continuing their valuation method while avoiding the high valuations that would result from the use of current unit prices. Such commissions found the use of average prices particularly appropriate for this purpose. The change from reproduction cost at current unit prices to reproduction cost at average unit prices was in form not very great, but in effect was of tremendous importance. The earlier use of average unit prices had accustomed courts, commissions, and utility companies to this method of valuation, so that its later use did not seem to be too great an innovation. Valuation at average unit prices had been a widely accepted practice before the war; it became an almost universally accepted practice during and after the war. Even utility companies were not hostile to the early wartime use of average prices. In the valuations they submitted to commissions in 1917 and 1918 they frequently made use of average unit prices in computing their estimates of the reproduction cost of their property.

It was not difficult to justify the use of average unit prices in the war period. The temporary and abnormal conditions that rendered unfair a reproduction cost valuation at current prices in ordinary times were even more extreme in wartime, and the need for average unit prices was, therefore, greater. The doctrine of fair value, which is the basis of the rate making rule, became under war conditions a doctrine of normal value. With normal value accepted as the proper meaning of fair value, the reproduction cost method of valuation at average unit prices came into general use. Its development from 1917 to 1921 embraced three phases: the extension of the method to states that had formerly used reproduction cost at current prices, the standardization of the five-year period for average prices, and the application of this method of valuation in all rate making cases in many states.

The extension of the use of reproduction cost valuation at average unit prices began early in 1917 with the rather hesitant use of three- and four-year average prices by commissions that had formerly used current prices. The Brooklyn Borough Gas case, July, 1918, was especially helpful in extending the use of average unit prices. In this case the company submitted a valuation based on reproduction cost at average prices for the five years ending in 1916. Chief Justice Hughes, then referee for the New York Supreme Court, rejected the proposed valuation as too high. He pointed out that the company's expert "properly shrank from predicating the validity of rates on a hypothetical cost of reproduction on December 31, 1916. . . . His endeavor was to get at a basis for rate making by seeking a fair reproduction value based on a period of five years and thus to avoid what he regarded as an abnormal reproduction cost" (P. U. R. 1918 F, 348). With Mr. Hughes rejecting reproduction cost at five-year average prices as excessive, utility companies could not very well complain of unfair treatment if commissions were generous enough to base rates on a valuation determined in this manner.

Before 1918, average prices for a period of two to five years had been in general use, with the five-year period the most common. By 1918 the five-year period had become the standard because shorter period averages no longer succeeded in maintaining low rate making values. The California Commission, which had formerly used two- and three-year averages, in 1918 rejected a valuation submitted by a utility company based on four-year average prices, and accepted the valuation of its own engineers "based upon prices obtaining during the five years directly preceding the recent abnormal increase due to war conditions" (P. U. R. 1918 E, 563). The Illinois Commission had formerly used current prices, but in 1917 it began the use of three-year average prices, and in 1918 five-year average prices for reproduction cost valuations (P. U. R. 1918 D, 121). By the end of 1918, all commissions that used reproduction cost at average prices had accepted the five-year period as the most suitable for determining fair value.

In more than fifteen states, reproduction cost at five-year average prices was the principal method of valuation, and in some states it was for many years the only method of valuation commissions used. Before the war, the Indiana Commission had valued utility property at reproduction cost at current prices. During the war, the commission reversed its position and acknowledged the superiority of the prudent investment method of valuation. However, as the courts had expressed a preference for reproduction cost valuation, the Indiana Commission adopted this method, but after 1918 made use of it with five-year average unit prices. The commission held that the use of average prices, including the high prices of the war years, met the requirement of the first Consolidated Gas case, that a utility company must be given the benefit of a rise in the cost of reproducing its property. When prices continued to rise to unexpectedly high levels, the commission extended the period for which average prices were taken to ten years, and in some cases to an even longer period.[8]

The Public Service Companies Law of 1913 required the Pennsylvania Commission to use average prices in determining reproduction cost. Under the circumstances, the commission had merely to continue its previous method of valuation to avoid the high reproduction cost estimates that would result from the use of current prices. In applying its policy of reproduction cost at five-year average prices, the Pennsylvania Commission developed an interesting procedure. Engineers representing the utility company, the consumers, and the commission were formed into a conference which reported fair unit prices for a five-year period prescribed by the commission. These conferences were a great aid in minimizing controversy, but they did not entirely eliminate litigation, for utilities were not bound to accept the valuations of the conferences. The first valuation conference

[8] For the use of average unit prices in reproduction cost valuations in Indiana, see the following cases: *Re United Public Service Co.*, P. U. R. 1918 F, 316; *Re Citizens' Telephone Co.*, P. U. R. 1919 B, 353; *Re Home Telephone Co.*, P. U. R. 1919 C, 209; *Re Central Union Telephone Co.*, P. U. R. 1920 B, 813; *Re Union Telephone Co.*, P. U. R., 1920 F, 391. See also, *Re Indianapolis Water Co.*, P. U. R. 1917 E, 556.

was used in the Spring Water case, in 1919, in which a five-year average to 1917 was made the basis for determining unit prices. The Pennsylvania Commission continued to use reproduction cost at five-year average prices of 1913 to 1917 until late in 1920, when it turned to the use of ten-year averages in order to find lower valuations than had become possible with reproduction cost at five-year average prices.[4]

3. TEN-YEAR AVERAGE PRICES

With the decline in the price level in 1920 and 1921, five-year average unit prices exceeded current unit prices in all utility industries. By 1919 it had already become apparent that average unit prices for the five preceding years were no longer successful in maintaining low rate making values. In order to minimize the effect of high average unit prices, commissions used two devices, neither of which was entirely satisfactory. In some rate cases, the property was valued at five-year average prices of a period antedating the great wartime inflation; and in other rate cases, commissions arbitrarily reduced valuations based on five-year average prices because they were excessive.

The reduction of valuations based on average unit prices was never a common practice, but it occurred often enough to be recognized as one method of offsetting high average prices. In the Home Telephone case, in 1919, the Indiana Commission reduced the valuation at five-year average prices by one-ninth because it unduly reflected the abnormally high war costs of materials and supplies (P. U. R. 1919 C, 214). The Arkansas Commission, in 1920, reduced a valuation at five-year average

[4] Conferences on valuation had been used by the Illinois Commission, P. U. R. 1917 E, 288, and by the New Jersey Commission, P. U. R. 1918 A, 178, prior to the hearing in *Borough of Kane v. Spring Water Co.* (Penna.), P. U. R. 1919 C, 404. The Pennsylvania Commission, however, was the only one to continue the use of valuation conferences. M. L. Cooke, *Public Utility Regulation*, p. 238. On the use of average unit prices in Pennsylvania, see the following cases: *Moore v. Valley Railways Co.*, P. U. R. 1919 F, 493; *Borough of Scottdale v. Citizens' Water Co.*, P. U. R. 1920 D, 292; *Township of Whitehall v. Clear Spring Water Co.*, P. U. R. 1920 E, 284; *Borough of Plymouth v. Wilkesbarre Railway Co.*, P. U. R. 1920 F, 677; *Borough of Verona v. Suburban Water Co.*, P. U. R. 1920 F, 942.

Reproduction Cost at Current and Average Prices*

Year	Street Railways			Light and Power			Artificial Gas		
	Current Prices	5-Year Av.	10-Year Av.	Current Prices	5-Year Av.	10-Year Av.	Current Prices	5-Year Av.	10-Year Av.
1914...........	97	...	...	92	...	...	97	...	...
1915...........	100	...	...	99	...	...	100	...	...
1916.............	120	...	...	128	...	...	133	...	...
1917...........	163	116	...	163	116	...	191	124	...
1918...........	192	134	...	177	132	...	211	146	...
1919...........	205	156	...	182	150	...	222	171	...
1920...........	245	185	142	211	172	135	264	204	151
1921...........	201	201	152	182	183	143	203	218	162
1922...........	175	204	160	161	183	149	192	218	171
1923...........	200	205	170	179	183	157	223	221	184

*1913=100. Adapted from L. R. Nash, *The Economics of Public Utilities*, 2nd edition, p. 183.

prices by one-twelfth because some of the unit costs entering into the valuation were too high (P. U. R. 1920 D, 755). Similar instances occurred in other states. Reductions of this sort obviously could not be made the basis for a valuation policy. In fact, the practice was a departure from the theory of normal reproduction cost on which the use of average unit prices was based. If five-year average prices were not normal, there could be no particular reason for their use.

A more usual device for avoiding high average prices was to choose a five-year period antedating the postwar rise in the price level. The Maine Commission and the Pennsylvania Commission, for example, used the average prices of 1913 to 1917 in valuations they made as late as 1920. Although the use of five-year average prices for a period three or more years before the date of a valuation succeeded in maintaining low rate making values, it seemed more appropriate for determining past than present normal reproduction cost. For this reason utility companies claimed that this use of average unit prices was not in accord with the present value principle, even if present value is defined as present normal value.

With continued high prices it was futile to look to the past for justification for low valuations. Clearly enough, the view that high war prices would be a temporary phenomenon had been mistaken. It could still be said, of course, that the higher price level was temporary in the sense that a lower price level might be expected in the future, and that an average of prices for a period longer than five years would approximate this future level of prices. This point of view was well expressed by the Vermont Commission in the Montpelier Electric case (P. U. R. 1920 E, 558):

> We are of the opinion that reproduction new with unit costs as of the present would not be an equitable method of determining fair value to be considered in fixing rates for future application. Neither do we think it fair to consider reproduction new based upon prices current in the prewar period. Assuming that prices are at the present time approximately at the peak and that the future decline is likely to be in some degree comparable to the past rise in prices, we are of the opinion that a valuation based upon average prices for a period of ten years, including the war period, ought to produce as fair results as it is possible to arrive at.

The expected lower price level of the future was in this way used to justify the use of ten-year average prices. It should be added that some commissions said that inasmuch as rate schedules were intended for application in the future, it was proper that the expected future level of prices should determine the rate making value.

In 1921, when the first postwar price decline set in, current unit costs for reproducing utility property were less than five-year average unit costs. Commissions were faced with the problem of returning to current reproduction cost valuation or extending the period for taking average prices to ten years. In favor of ten-year average prices it could be said that their use had been recommended in the *Valuation Brief of 1915*, and that this recommendation had been followed in part by the Interstate Commerce Commission. Several state commissions had also made occasional use of ten-year average prices in valuations in 1917 and later.[5] The deciding consideration in favor of their

---

[5] *Re Monroe Independent Telephone Co.* (Neb.), P. U. R. 1917 E, 471; *Re Moore Park Water, Light & Power Co.* (Calif.), P. U. R. 1919 B, 679; *Re Springfield Water Co.* (Mo.), P. U. R. 1919 D, 853; *Re United Fuel Gas Co.* (W. Va.), P. U. R. 1920 C, 853; *Re Litchfield Water Supply Co.* (Ill.), P. U. R. 1920 D, 332; *Re Rogers Light & Water Co.* (Ark.), P. U. R. 1920 E, 311.

use, however, was the fact that ten-year average prices made possible valuations much below those that would result from the use of reproduction cost at current prices.

Reproduction cost at ten-year average prices was most extensively used in Pennsylvania and in Indiana. The Pennsylvania Commission had used five-year averages until 1920. To avoid the high valuations necessitated by the use of this method of determining unit costs, the commission extended the period over which prices were averaged to ten years. This was the method the Pennsylvania Commission used in the valuation cases it decided from 1921 to 1923.[6] However, the increasing emphasis on reproduction cost at current prices in several court decisions caused the commission to abandon the use of average unit prices entirely in 1924. In the York Water case, the commission took evidence of reproduction cost on the basis of average unit prices, but the final rate making value was fixed at current reproduction cost. The commission said: "While these ten- and five-year estimates have not been entirely disregarded, the Commission has given a great deal more consideration to the remaining reproduction studies, and particularly, in the light of decisions of the courts, to the estimate of present day reproduction cost, depreciated" (P. U. R. 1924 C, 680).

The most important use of reproduction cost valuation at ten-year average prices was by the Indiana Commission, particularly in the Indianapolis Water cases. In 1917 the commission valued the Indianapolis Water Co. at ten-year average prices for materials and at current prices for labor. In a valuation of the same property, in 1923, the commission used unit prices based on ten-year averages of labor and material costs. At a rehearing later that year the commission refused to increase its valuation. How firmly it was fixed in its valuation policy is seen from the report in this case (P. U. R. 1924 B, 327-328).

Throughout the year 1922 in all valuation cases before this Commission, and in Cause No. 6613, *supra*, valuations of physical prop-

[6] *Borough of Brockville v. Mound City Water Co.*, P. U. R. 1921 C, 820; *Belle Vernon v. Belle Vernon Water Co.*, P. U. R. 1923 B, 193; *Re Kittanning Telephone Co.*, P. U. R. 1923 B, 842; *Re Borough of Wrightsville*, P. U. R. 1923 C, 705.

erty approximated the results of applying the 10-year average cost for the last preceding and completed ten years, depreciated to present condition. No radical departure from the general manner of handling cases at the time was made in said cause, but it was placed upon practically the same grounds as other valuation investigations conducted during the preceding year. The Commission had in mind the various elements to be considered as laid down in the case of *Smyth v. Ames,* and approved in many later decisions of the United States Supreme Court, and had in mind the probable general trend of prices and believed at the time that the 10-year appraisal made by the engineering staff was incidentally approximately the value of the property and would be the value for some time to come.

This valuation was later held to be confiscatory by the Supreme Court. It should be noted that the Indiana Commission made some use of average prices for periods as long as fifteen and twenty years. After 1924 the commission made no use of long period average prices, undoubtedly because the decisions of the courts indicated that wartime methods of valuation would no longer be regarded as conforming to the rate making rule.[7]

4. THE ATTITUDE OF THE COURTS

Until 1920 commissions were highly successful in their use of reproduction cost at average unit prices. Not only were valuations kept low by this method, but commissions were little disturbed by litigation. The acquiescence of utility companies in the use of five-year average prices was partly due to the expectation that the courts would sustain the legality of this valuation method, and partly to the recognition that the use of five-year average prices did no great injustice to utility companies. In 1918, while the war was still on, there could be little hope for successful litigation, particularly in view of the report of Chief

[7] For ten-year averages, see *Re Northern Indiana Gas & Electric Co.,* P. U. R. 1919 F, 567; *Re Lafayette Telephone Co.,* P. U. R. 1920 A, 422; *Re Indiana General Service Co.,* P. U. R. 1920 A, 489; *City of Fort Wayne v. Home Telephone & Telegraph Co.,* P. U. R. 1920 D, 83. For Indianapolis Water cases, see P. U. R. 1917 E, 556; P. U. R. 1923 D, 449; P. U. R. 1924 B, 306; and the discussion in section 4, below. For longer period averages, see *Re Southern Indiana Telephone & Telegraph Co.,* P. U. R. 1921 E, 142; *Brookville v. Brookville Electric Co.,* P. U. R. 1922 D, 1; *Re City of Vincennes,* P. U. R. 1924 B, 571.

Justice Hughes as referee in the Brooklyn Borough Gas case. In 1919 and 1920, five-year average prices were almost as high as current prices, so that the inducement to contest such valuations had almost disappeared.

When valuations involving the use of five-year average prices were taken to the courts, it was the period chosen rather than the method itself that was regarded as unfair. With few exceptions state courts held such valuations to be illegal. Among the most influential of state court cases was that of the Elizabethtown Gaslight Co. The New Jersey Commissioners had valued the property of the utility company acquired before 1918 at the average unit prices for the five years preceding 1916. The valuation was contested on the ground that the unit prices were too low. In 1920, the state Supreme Court upheld the constitutional right of the company to have its property valued at the prices prevailing at the time of the appraisal. The court said that "the failure to allow for prices at the time to which the rates apply, July 1, 1919, was an error. It is not denied that prices were very much higher in 1919, and are very much higher now, than the average for the years 1911 to 1916" (P. U. R. 1920 F, 1003). The decision was widely cited as authority for the use of current unit prices, even when very high.[8]

Ultimately, the use of five- and ten-year average prices depended on the attitude of the federal courts, for state courts did not pretend to exercise independent judgment on methods of valuation. Almost without exception, the federal courts held that the use of average prices was not in accord with the rate making rule as interpreted by the Supreme Court. An important federal court decision on this question was that of Judge Learned Hand in the second Consolidated Gas case, 1920. A special master had held for the company in its plea to have the New York Eighty Cents Gas law set aside as confiscatory. The state asked the court to disregard the recommendation of the

[8] State courts rejected valuations at average prices also in *Coal District Power Co. v. Booneville* (Ark.), P. U. R. 1924 B, 726; *Michigan Public Utilities Commission v. Michigan State Telephone Co.* (Mich.), P. U. R. 1925 C, 158. The New Hampshire Supreme Court upheld the use of average prices in *Plymouth Electric Power Co. v. State*, P. U. R. 1923 E, 83.

master, and showed that the rate yielded a fair return on the property valued at average prices for the ten years after 1909. In denying the state's request, Judge Hand said (P. U. R. 1920 F, 487-488):

The defendants wish me . . . to take an average over the whole period [since 1909] both for the cost of production and capital valuation. Now whatever may be the proper method, that certainly is wrong. The case is not one in which an average can safely be made, because the variations in price which the whole period covers are not normally recurrent. Averages pre-suppose that the resulting figure will cover variations which, though certain or nearly certain within the period taken, are impossible of exact prediction in their occurrence. They may,, therefore, be spread over a period precisely as an insurance loss is spread. The recent rise in prices is not of this kind, because there is no reason whatever to suppose that during the next period of say five years, which is long enough to justify some present actions, the same causes will operate in reverse as have operated in the past. An average would be, therefore, meaningless.

Judge Hand further defended the use of current reproduction cost on the ground that it involved no hardship for consumers. With the decreased purchasing power of the dollar, a higher level of rates could not be regarded as a burden to the consumer or a boon to the utility investor. The decision holding the rate confiscatory was sustained by the Supreme Court, although it did not pass on the valuation (P. U. R. 1922 B, 752).

The most important case in which the courts passed judgment on the use of average prices in valuation was unquestionably that of the Indianapolis Water Co. The Indiana Commission valued the property of the company at ten-year average prices, emphasizing that this had been for some time the policy of the commission. In 1924, the Federal District Court ruled that the valuation was confiscatory, and that current reproduction cost must be given dominant consideration in determining rate making value (P. U. R. 1925 A, 740). On appeal to the Supreme Court, the findings of the district court were sustained. Justice Butler, in the opinion for the court, said (P. U. R. 1927 A, 24):

The validity of the rates in question depends on the property value January 1, 1924, and for a reasonable time following. While the values of such properties do not vary with frequent minor fluctuations in the prices of material and labor required to produce them, they are affected by and generally follow the relatively permanent level and trend of such prices. . . . And we may take judicial notice of the fact that there has been no substantial general decline in the prices of labor and materials since that time. The trend has been upward rather than downward. The price level adopted by the Commission—the average for ten years ending with 1921—was too low.

The court's view that reproduction cost at current prices was equivalent to rate making value was effective in terminating the use of all valuation methods other than that based on current reproduction cost.

5. Some Objections Considered

The principal merit of reproduction cost valuation at average prices was the ease with which its use was established. Commissions held that this method of valuation did not depart from the fundamental principles of the rate making rule. It was not denied that the present value of the property must be fixed as the rate base, and that reproduction cost was the best indication of present value. Commissions simply interpreted reproduction cost to mean normal reproduction cost. The continued use of the dilatory and expensive prewar valuation procedure —the inventory, unit prices, and deduction of observable depreciation—did not contribute to efficient administration. However, without this procedure it might not have been possible to use average prices, for utility companies regarded the procedure as a safeguard against arbitrary valuations, and many courts required the procedure for compliance with the constitutional provision for due process. On the whole, the low rate making valuations and the limited litigation prior to 1920 indicate the soundness of the policy of using reproduction cost at average unit prices in wartime valuation.

The early use of average prices did not invite opposition from utility companies. The higher prices of the war years were included in the averages, and there was an implied assurance that after five years they would be of dominant importance, or if prices should decline, the use of current prices would be resumed. It was clear, therefore, that the use of average prices could not long maintain valuations below the level of current reproduction cost, unless bias in favor of consumers was deliberately introduced. For these reasons, utility companies acquiesced in the use of average prices, particularly as insistence on valuation at current prices during the war might incur the hostility of the community and open the way to a charge of profiting by a public calamity. Besides, there was no assurance that the courts would sustain their right to valuation at the high current prices of wartime.

The justification for the use of average prices was the assumption that the prevailing price level was abnormal and temporary. It was thought that the use of average unit prices would eliminate the temporary abnormalities and prepare the way for a return to the prewar method of valuation—reproduction cost at current prices. It was expected that five years after the war, say by 1923, prices would be sufficiently below the war level to be regarded as normal. This view of the probable movement of prices was supported by elaborate studies of prices during and after the Civil War. By 1921 it had become apparent that the postwar price level, although high, was not temporary. To offset the effect of continued high prices on valuation, the period for averages was extended to ten years. This innovation was not acceptable to the courts, and after the postwar plateau in prices became evident, the hypothetical basis for the use of average prices in reproduction cost valuation disappeared.

One of the great disadvantages of valuation at average prices was the obvious inadequacy of this method as a permanent plan for valuation. Reproduction cost at average unit prices, regardless of the length of the period for which average prices are taken, must ultimately exceed current reproduction cost when prices begin to decline. If valuations are not to become excessively high, the length of the average period must be continually varied, or the method must be abandoned. This was the general experience of commissions that used this method of valuation. "The tendency," said the Indiana Commission, "towards the application of two-, five-, ten-year, or any averages, to this method of evaluation, emphasizes its character as a makeshift substitute and discloses its weakness" (P. U. R. 1919 A, 448). By its nature, reproduction cost at average unit prices was certain to result in a return to current reproduction cost as the measure of rate making value, once some degree of price stability was attained. It was incapable, therefore, of terminating the long existing controversy on valuation.

A more important objection to this method of valuation was its tendency to penalize those utility companies that were compelled to expand their facilities to meet war needs. In general, wartime construction was kept at a minimum. Those utility enterprises that did undertake new construction during the war were the ones most economically situated and most efficiently managed. In using average unit prices to value utility property, regardless of the time of acquisition or construction, commissions placed such efficient utility companies in a less favorable position after expansion than before. A utility that undertook new construction in 1918 would have found that its new investment was worth less than three-fourths of the actual cost if the property was valued at five-year average prices. The difficulty is inherent in the use of averages. "It seems apparent," said the West Virginia Commission, "that it would be extremely difficult, if not impossible, to find an average unit cost that would be fairly applicable to construction made in part at prewar and in part at war prices, especially if the same is to be of value as a basis for future rate making" (P. U. R. 1921 B, 108). In the conventions of utility operators in 1923 and 1924, great stress was placed on the necessity of protecting investments made at high prices by order of state commissions.[9] The failure to differentiate property constructed at high wartime prices from property constructed at low prewar prices was the outstanding weakness of valuation at average unit prices.

[9] See the reports of the Valuation Committee of the American Electric Railway Association, *Proceedings,* 1923, p. 187; *Proceedings,* 1924, pp. 17 ff.

CHAPTER VI

VALUATION: THE USE OF CORRECTIVE INDICES

1. Reasonable and Normal Appreciation

THE PRIMARY OBJECT of valuation in the war and postwar periods was to give some recognition to higher current prices while avoiding valuations as high as reproduction cost at current prices. Another object of valuation in the war and postwar periods was to avoid the dilatory and expensive prewar valuation procedure. The corrective index method of valuation was well suited to attain these objects. Where a basic valuation at prewar prices was available, the present value could be determined without difficulty by applying an index of present fair value. This index, if chosen for the purpose, could be made to fix a rate base higher than reproduction cost at prewar prices, but lower than reproduction cost at current prices.

The use of corrective indices began with the addition of a small percentage, from 5 to 20 per cent, to valuations based on prewar prices to allow for the higher prices of the war period. In several states, commissions increased the valuations they made by a small percentage because the prices used clearly were not fair.[1] In these instances the usual method of valuation—say, reproduction cost at average prices—did not, for some reason, sufficiently reflect higher current prices. The addition of 5 to 20 per cent to the basic valuation served to prevent the injustice that would result if the usual method of valuation had been applied. The use of a corrective index was not the distinctive feature of these valuations. However, from this early use of a small additional percentage was developed the later use of the corrective index method of valuation, in which basic valuations at prewar prices were corrected by application of an index number of reasonable, normal, or present prices.

[1] See, for example, *Re Potomac Electric Power Co.* (D. C.), P. U. R. 1917 D, 563; *Re United Railways Co.* (Mo.), P. U. R. 1918 D, 392; *Re City of Redding* (Calif.), P. U. R. 1919 F, 415.

Prior to 1921 the New Jersey Commission valued utility property by applying five-year average prewar prices to property acquired before the war. The state Supreme Court held that such valuations gave no recognition to high current prices and were, therefore, unconstitutional. The commission then modified its policy to the extent of increasing such valuations by the use of an index reflecting the reasonable increase in construction costs. The policy of reasonable appreciation is well illustrated by the valuation in the Coast Gas case, 1922. A valuation made at 1913 and 1914 prices was increased by 30 per cent to give the estimated average cost of reproduction predicted for the five years from 1922 to 1926 (P. U. R. 1923 A, 349). The corrective index was determined by a rather complex method. The price trend was projected from 1893 to 1926 on the basis of the average annual increase in prices from 1893 to 1914. The index number of prices by this trend method was averaged with the Bureau of Labor Statistics index number of wholesale prices. The final index, 130 on the prewar base, was made the reasonable corrective index to be applied to the basic valuation. Until the resumption of current reproduction cost valuation, the New Jersey Commission used such corrective indices to increase basic valuations at prewar prices to their reasonable present value.

Quite similar was the development of the policy of normal appreciation by the Virginia Corporation Commission. Until 1921 the commission valued utility property acquired before the war at five-year average prewar prices. When the state Supreme Court of Appeals refused to sustain such valuations, the commission adopted the policy of allowing normal appreciation in construction costs. The principle was formulated in the Virginia Railway & Power valuation, in 1921. The basic valuation was at 1914 prices, and to this the commission added its estimate of normal appreciation. "Had there been no war," said the commission, "there would have been a gradual rise in prices due to increasing costs of production. Thus we have a basis which allows the company the benefit of appreciating values in normal times, based on prewar values, plus actual additions made at war prices" (P. U. R. 1921 C, 193). As this normal appreciation was estimated to be 2 per cent, later 3 per cent, annually, the policy in practice gave little recognition to high current prices. Thus, in the Lynchburg Traction case, 1921, the normal appreciation was fixed at 10.8 per cent—2 per cent annually compounded for five years—which was added to the reproduction cost at 1916 prices (P. U. R. 1921 E, 87). At this time the construction cost index for street railways was 60 per cent, and for electric power companies 40 per cent, above the 1916 level.

The Virginia Supreme Court of Appeals rejected valuations in which a corrective index of 10 and 20 per cent were used, but it held that an appreciation of 40 per cent gave due consideration to reproduction cost at current prices as required by the present value principle (P. U. R. 1925 A, 769). The policy of normal appreciation was never approved as such by the state Supreme Court of Appeals. The court concerned itself entirely with the question whether sufficient consideration was given to reproduction cost at present prices. It was only when the index of normal appreciation gave this recognition to current prices that the court approved a valuation. In many instances corrective index valuations by the commission were held to be too low, and for this reason the commission increased its normal corrective index from 10 per cent to 40 per cent. Finally, as in other states, when the courts insisted that present value was equivalent to reproduction cost at current prices, the Virginia Commission abandoned the use of corrective indices in valuation.

2. CORRECTIVE INDEX VALUATION IN MISSOURI

The corrective index method of valuation was more extensively used in Missouri than in any other state. Before 1920 the Missouri Commission used reproduction cost at five-year average prices in its valuations; but after 1921, when five-year average prices exceeded current prices, the commission changed to actual investment cost as the measure of the rate base. In several instances utility companies requested the commission to increase its investment cost valuations to give some recognition to higher postwar prices. In 1921, the Macon Telephone Co. and the Home Telephone Co. of Joplin requested the commission to value their property by increasing prewar cost valuations by 60 per cent, a request that was refused. In 1922 the utility companies modified their demands, and requested that prewar cost valuations be increased by 33 1/3 per cent, a formula that had been used by the Federal District Court in Texas (see section 3, below). The commission rejected this request, holding that prices would decline, and cited as evidence the fall in construction costs from 1920 to 1922.

A change in the commission's valuation policy was inevitable. The rise in prices in 1922 led to successful litigation of commission valuations. The Federal District Court had already set aside two valuations of the Missouri Commission for failure to give adequate consideration to current prices (267 Fed. 584; P. U. R. 1921 A, 540), and the Southwestern Bell Telephone case was then pending in the Supreme Court. In the meantime, the federal courts were giving their approval to the use of corrective indices in valuation. In 1922 the Missouri Commission reversed its former policy and increased a valuation at prewar prices by 33 1/3 per cent to give weight to higher current prices (P. U. R. 1922 E, 805). In 1923, after the federal courts approved the use of higher corrective indices, the commission increased the basic prewar cost valuations by 50 per cent (P. U. R. 1923 D, 332).

The Supreme Court's decision in the Southwestern Bell Telephone case in 1923 was an important factor leading to the extensive use of corrective indices by the Missouri Commission. When federal operation of the telephone industry was terminated in 1919, the commission issued an order reducing rates to a level sufficient to yield a fair return on a valuation at prewar prices. The order was sustained in the state courts, but was set aside as confiscatory by the Supreme Court. The commission had justified its valuation on the ground that lower prices could be expected in the future. On this the Supreme Court said: "It is impossible to ascertain what will amount to a fair return upon the properties devoted to public service without giving consideration to the cost of labor, supplies, etc., at the time the investigation is made. . . . Estimates for tomorrow cannot ignore prices of today." (262 U. S. 276, 287).

The effect of this decision was to induce the commission to make use of higher corrective indices. In several cases basic valuations at prewar prices were increased by 50 per cent to allow for greater current costs.[2] Ultimately, however, the commission was required to return to the use of reproduction cost at current prices as the measure of rate making value. In 1924 the Federal District Court set aside a valuation of the Joplin Gas Co. based on prewar cost increased by 50 per cent, on the ground that the commission had given insufficient consideration to current prices (P. U. R. 1924 D, 137). Again in 1925 a valuation of the Springfield Gas & Electric Co. was set aside by the Federal District Court, and the commission was ordered to give greater recognition to reproduction cost at current prices in its valuations (P. U. R. 1926 C, 858). Thereafter the commission gave up the use of corrective indices. In 1928, however, in a valuation of the street railways of St. Louis, the commission used a weighted index of construction costs taken from the *Engineering News-Record.* The full indicated increase in construction costs was allowed (P. U. R. 1928 E, 419).

3. CORRECTIVE INDEX VALUATION BY FEDERAL COURTS

The use of the corrective index method of valuation received considerable impetus from the custom of the federal courts of comparing commission valuations, usually at prewar prices, with current construction costs to determine their fairness. Where a considerable difference existed between reproduction cost at prewar prices and at current prices, the courts on occasion held that present fair value could be determined by increasing the commission valuation—say, by 50 per cent. The use of this method by Judge Hutcheson of the Federal District Court of Texas in the Houston Electric case (P. U. R. 1920 F, 328), and especially in the Galveston case, was influential in bringing about a wide

[2] See, for example, *Re United Railways Co. of St. Louis,* P. U. R. 1923 D, 759; *Re Missouri Electric Railroad Co.,* P. U. R. 1923 D, 851. In *Re Home Telephone Co.,* P. U. R. 1924 A, 253, the commission allowed an increase of 44 per cent rather than the customary 50 per cent of the basic valuation.

acceptance of this method of valuation by commissions and by courts in other states.

The Galveston City Commission fixed the street car fare for that city at five cents. The Galveston Electric Co. applied for an injunction restraining the city from enforcing the fare. The Federal District Court did not grant an injunction, but appointed a master to take evidence as to the fair value of the utility's property and the sufficiency of the fare. The master held that the proper basis for determining the rate value was the probable future level of prices. The agreed cost at prewar prices was therefore made basic, and evidence was introduced on probable future prices. At this time, 1921, construction costs were 110 per cent above 1913 prices. The utility company contended that prices would finally settle at 60 to 70 per cent above the prewar level. The city commission contended that prices would return to approximately the 1913 level. The master recommended that the basic value be increased by 33 1/3 per cent, a recommendation accepted by the court. Additions since the basic valuation were included at actual cost. On appeal to the Supreme Court, the valuation of the special master was sustained (P. U. R. 1922 D, 159).

In addition to these decisions of Judge Hutcheson, two cases in the federal courts of Minnesota aided in bringing the corrective index method of valuation into wider use. In 1919 the City of Winona valued the property of the Wisconsin-Minnesota Light & Power Co. on the basis of average prices for the fifteen years from 1900 to 1914. To give consideration to present prices, the basic valuation was increased by 25 per cent. The utility company contended that the increase allowed was insufficient, and it was sustained in this contention by the Federal District Court (P. U. R. 1921 A, 146). In 1921 the case again came before the court and the matter was referred to a special master for determination of the rate making value. The master recommended a valuation at reproduction cost at 1919 prices. The court rejected the master's recommendation, and said that reproduction cost at current prices was not the measure of rate making value (P. U. R. 1922 C, 461).

These decisions were synthesized when the Circuit Court of Appeals decided that a rate making value 50 per cent above a basic valuation at prewar prices would be fair for the Minneapolis Gas Co. The case had come to the Federal District Court on an injunction proceeding to restrain the enforcement of a city ordinance fixing gas rates. The court appointed a master to report on the fair rate making value. The master found the fair value by increasing the actual prewar cost by 25 per cent to allow for higher current prices. The report was confirmed by the court and both parties appealed. The Circuit Court of Appeals in its decision, 1923, held that an allowance of 25 per cent failed to give adequate weight to reproduction cost at prices prevailing at the time of the valuation. Judge Munger, for the court, said that "no marked recession of prices has taken place since the time this case was heard by the master, and there is no present appearance of an assured reduction. Our conclusion is that the master's increase of the undepreciated cost price . . . is too low, and that this base should be increased by 50 per cent" (285 Fed. 827). The Minneapolis decision was widely cited by commissions and courts as authority for the use of a corrective index of 50 per cent. Inasmuch as the construction cost index for gas utilities at the time was 120 per cent above the 1913 level, the decision of the court did not give great weight to current prices, unless the property was abnormally depreciated.

The corrective index method of valuation became increasingly popular after 1923 largely because it offered a plan for avoiding prewar valuation procedure with reproduction cost at current prices as the dominant element in the rate base. The acceptability of the corrective index method of valuation to the federal courts was an additional recommendation. In fact, in 1923 the federal courts seem to have been favorably impressed by the possibility of avoiding the difficulties of valuation procedure by the use of corrective indices. Judge Farrington had this to say of the corrective index method of valuation: "If it were possible to find with confidence the original cost of the plant and of subsequent additions thereto, . . . some light

might be afforded as to present reasonable value by applying to
the original cost a percentage factor which represents the difference between present prices and those prevailing during the
period of construction" (P. U. R. 1923 E, 485).

The general attitude of the federal courts toward the use of
corrective indices continued to be favorable in 1924 and 1925.
After the Georgia decision in the Supreme Court (chapter VII,
section 5, below), the case again reached the Federal District
Court in 1924, and a special master was appointed to report on
fair rate making value. The master held that if a corrective index of 60 per cent were applied to a 1914 valuation, and additions
since then also adjusted to current prices, a fair value would be
determined. The valuation on this basis was upheld by the
court (P. U. R. 1925 A, 546). The index of construction costs
for utilities was then 100 per cent above 1914 prices, so that the
application of a corrective index of 60 per cent by the court was
regarded as approval of valuation methods in which reproduction cost at current prices was not given dominant recognition.

Later in 1924, another corrective index valuation was made
by the Federal District Court of Minnesota. The Duluth Street
Railways applied to the court to enjoin the enforcement of a
rate order of the Minnesota Commission. The court appointed a
special master to report on the fair value of the company's property. The master took a basic valuation at prewar prices and
added to this an appreciation of 21 per cent to allow for higher
prevailing prices. The court did not accept the valuation because
the corrective index the master used gave insufficient consideration to current prices. Instead, the court applied a corrective index of 40 per cent to the basic valuation (P. U. R. 1925 D, 226).
At this time the index of street railway construction costs was
more than 100 per cent above the 1913 level.

For a final illustration of the use of a corrective index by a
federal court, the Maryland telephone case may be cited. The
Maryland Commission valued the property of the utility company on the basis of 1914 prices, with wartime construction valued
at actual cost (P. U. R. 1925 B, 545). In 1925 the case reached
the Circuit Court of Appeals where the valuation was held to

be confiscatory. The court said that a fair rate base could be determined by correcting the commission's valuation by the indicated rise in wholesale prices shown by the Bureau of Labor Statistics index (P. U. R. 1925 D, 407). At the time of the commission's valuation in 1924, wholesale prices were 50 per cent above the 1913 level, while telephone construction costs were 70 per cent above the 1913 level. The use of wholesale prices instead of telephone construction costs thus resulted in a rate base below reproduction cost at current prices.

4. DISAPPROVAL OF INDICES BY THE FEDERAL COURTS

The emphasis of the courts on current reproduction cost, indicated in part in the previous chapter, led ultimately to the abandonment of the corrective index method of valuation. The Mobile Gas case was one of the first in which a federal court disapproved the use of a corrective index. The property of the utility company was valued by the Alabama Commission at prewar prices with 50 per cent of the basic valuation added to allow for the higher level of current prices. The case was carried to the Federal District Court where the valuation was held to be confiscatory. The court said that to value "a utility for rate making purposes by valuing its property at prewar prices, and then adding thereto one-half of the increase in prices between that time and the time of the valuation, . . . is nothing more nor less than an effort to confiscate so much of the company's property as is represented by one-half of the increase in market values between the war period and the present time" (P. U. R. 1924 B, 644).

The insistence of the courts after 1924 on the predominant importance of reproduction cost at current prices was reflected in their attitude toward the use of corrective indices. The valuations made by the federal courts showed a steady rise in the corrective index that was regarded as necessary to give present value. While in 1920 a corrective index of 33 1/3 per cent of the basic prewar value was regarded as adequate, in 1924, a corrective index of 60 per cent of the basic prewar value was held to be inadequate. The decisions of the Federal District Court of Missouri in the Joplin and Springfield cases foreshadowed the end of corrective index valuation (P. U. R. 1924 D, 137; P. U. R. 1926 C, 858), for nowhere was this method of valuation more thoroughly established than in Missouri.

In the Monroe Gas case a valuation based on a corrective index was conclusively rejected by the courts. In 1924 the Michigan Commission valued the company's property at average prices for 1905 to 1914, and increased the basic valuation by 60 per cent to allow for higher prevailing prices. The corrective index was determined in the following manner: the ten-year average of prices from 1905 to 1914 was made basic, and from this an index of present construction costs was found by comparing with the base actual average prices paid for construction by the company since 1915. The index of actual average costs determined in this manner was approximately 160, while the index of current construction costs for gas utilities in 1924 was 220 on a 1913 base and even higher on the base used by the commission. The final valuation fixed by the commission was considerably less than present reproduction cost (P. U. R. 1924 C, 808).

This was unquestionably an extreme application of the corrective index method of valuation, and it was not surprising that the Federal District Court held it to be confiscatory. The court ruled that failure to give dominant consideration to reproduction cost at current prices deprived the utility company of its property without due process of law. In an earlier litigation involving the same company, the court had held that reproduction cost must be considered in determining fair value (P. U. R. 1923 E, 661). The court now went farther and said: "We think that the Supreme Court has now adopted the rule that, at least in the absence of special circumstances controlling otherwise, and not present here, the dominant element in the fixing of a rate base in a case such as is now before us is the reproduction cost" (P. U. R. 1926 D, 13). The opinion was widely cited, and the case became a leading authority against the use of wartime valuation methods. It should be noted, however, that the Supreme Court did not reject a corrective index valuation in this period.[3]

5. AN APPRAISAL OF CORRECTIVE INDEX VALUATION

Although the use of corrective indices was not as important a method of valuation as reproduction cost at average unit prices, it was probably superior for the purposes commissions had in view. Because of continued high prices, the use of averages had to be abandoned in 1921, at a time when the difficulties of valuation were still great. At this time commissions sought a valuation method that would minimize the complexity of prewar procedure and that would maintain valuations below reproduction cost at current prices. The corrective index method was admirably suited for these purposes. Not only could commissions dispense with the procedure that was ordinarily used in reproduction cost valuation at average prices, but by allowing only part of the indicated rise in construction costs they could avoid high valuations.

The great fluctuation in prices after the war intensified the valuation controversy from 1919 to 1925. Every considerable change in prices brought pressure from utility companies or consumers to revise rates. An examination of commission reports indicates the frequency with which revaluations were undertaken in this period. Under the circumstances, commissions were not equipped to undertake precise valuations. By the use of corrective indices, the former elaborate procedure could be avoided, for such valuations frequently started with a basic valuation already available. By applying to this basic valuation a corrective index that made allowance for higher prices, fair present value could be determined without great difficulty. Even when commissions did not intend to find a low rate making value, the corrective index method was used to simplify valuation procedure. Its usefulness for this purpose was widely recognized by the federal courts.

[a] During the recent depression the Supreme Court did reject a corrective index valuation in the Maryland telephone case, 8 P. U. R., N. S., 433. In fact, the index used in this case was the most elaborate the commission could devise for its purpose. See Chap. IX, section 4, below.

The corrective index method of valuation was unquestionably helpful in maintaining low rate making values. It is remarkable that at a time when utility companies were litigating valuations, and courts were emphasizing the importance of current prices, commissions succeeded in fixing low rate making values by use of this method. This was done by allowing less than the full rise in prices that would be shown by the use of accurate indices of utility construction costs. The final rate making value, when a corrective index was used, depended upon how the index was determined. Theoretically, the index showed the relation of fair prewar value to fair present value. In practice, various indices were used for this purpose. For simplicity, they may be classified in four groups: special indices designed for particular valuations, the Bureau of Labor Statistics index number of wholesale prices, indices of general construction costs, and indices of construction costs for particular utility industries. These groups of corrective indices will be considered in some detail.

(1). When a special index was used, it was not difficult to devise one that would result in a low valuation. Thus, in the Monroe Gas case, the Michigan Commission's index compared average prewar prices with average actual prices paid by the company from 1915 to 1924. The index of current construction costs for gas utilities in 1924 was 221 on a 1913 base, the index of ten-year average costs was 196 on the same base, and the index by the commission's method was 160. The special index used by the New Jersey Commission in the Coast Gas case is another example of this kind. The normal appreciation added to the basic valuation was found by averaging two indices—an index of normal prices found by extending the prewar price trend, and the Bureau of Labor Statistics index number of wholesale prices. The resulting index, 30 per cent above the 1913 base, allowed less than one-third of the increase in valuation that would have resulted from the use of current construction costs for gas utilities.

(2). The Bureau of Labor Statistics index number of wholesale prices was widely used in valuations, particularly to establish the nature of actual or hypothetical price movements. In some instances, as in the Maryland telephone case, the fair value for rate making was determined by converting a valuation at prewar prices into a present fair value by allowing the price rise shown by the index number of wholesale prices. In other instances, as in New Jersey and in Virginia, the Bureau of Labor Statistics index number was used to establish trends to determine normal or reasonable price changes. Because wholesale prices rose less than construction costs, the use of this index permitted commissions to fix valuations much below reproduction cost at current prices.

It was sometimes said by courts that allowing utility companies higher valuations did not result in giving them a return with greater purchasing power than they had before the price rise. Thus, Judge Hand in the second Consolidated Gas case said that an increased valuation adds nothing to the profits of the company, for while the profits are paid in more dollars, the dollars have proportionately less purchasing power (P. U. R. 1920 F, 483). A special master for the Federal District Court of Arkansas went so far as to say that "a dollar invested in a public utility shall be permitted to earn such income as will enable such income to buy the same amount of other things that the prevailing income on a dollar bought at the time the dollar was originally invested in the public utility" (P. U. R. 1924 C, 73). This theory would require that fair return be varied according to a retail price or cost of living index. In fact no use was made of cost of living indices, although some commissions regarded the wholesale price index as an approximate measure of the purchasing power of income. It should be noted that to allow utilities a constant real return during periods of high prices would permit utility common stockholders to receive an enlarged return in purchasing power, for the capital represented by bonds and preferred stock receives a constant money return.

(3). In Missouri and in other states the *Engineering News-Record* index of construction costs was frequently used in valuations. This index was based on the weighted average prices

CONSTRUCTION COSTS, WHOLESALE PRICES, AND RETAIL PRICES*

Year	Construction Costs	Wholesale Prices	Retail Prices
1914	88.6	98.1	102.7
1915	92.6	100.8	104.7
1916	129.6	126.8	116.6
1917	181.2	177.2	138.3
1918	189.2	194.3	166.9
1919	198.4	206.4	191.4
1920	251.3	226.2	195.6
1921	201.8	146.9	174.8
1922	174.4	148.8	170.3
1923	214.1	153.7	174.7
1924	215.4	149.7	174.3
1925	206.7	158.7	181.3

*1913=100. The construction costs index is from the *Engineering News-Record*, the wholesale and retail price indices are those of the Bureau of Labor Statistics.

of labor, steel, lumber, and cement. Because of the limited collection of commodities, this index could not be an accurate measure of construction costs for utilities. Further, differences in construction costs for various utilities were surprisingly large. In general, construction costs for gas and water companies rose much higher than construction costs for telephone, street railway, and electric power companies. For this reason use of the *Engineering News-Record* index of construction costs resulted in valuations above current reproduction cost for some utilities and below current reproduction cost for others. Despite these obvious deficiencies, the general construction costs index was very widely used.

(4). The index that most nearly represented reproduction cost at current prices was the construction costs index for a particular utility industry. Even with this index, inaccuracies were inevitable. Indices for construction costs for utility plants in the same industry might differ by as much as 20 per cent. Telephone construction costs, for example, cannot be expected to remain the same for companies operating under different conditions. The inventories of the property of the New York Telephone Co. and the Chapel Hill Telephone Co., to take an extreme instance, would differ considerably. Telephone poles and the cost of placing them would be an important item in Chapel Hill; they would be of minor importance in New York.

General and Particular Construction Costs*

Year	General Construction	Electric Power	Street Railways	Artificial Gas	Telephone	Water Works
1914.....	89	92	97	97	96	95
1915.....	93	99	100	100	101	99
1916.....	130	128	120	133	114	129
1917.....	181	163	163	191	135	197
1918.....	189	177	192	211	149	213
1919.....	198	182	201	222	166	212
1920.....	251	211	245	264	192	271
1921.....	202	182	202	203	184	220
1922.....	174	161	175	192	171	197
1923.....	214	179	200	223	177	234
1924.....	215	180	205	221	170	243

*1913=100. The construction costs index is from the *Engineering News-Record;* the electric power, street railway and artificial gas indices are from L. R. Nash, *Economics of Public Utilities,* 2nd edition, p. 183; the telephone and water works indices are from Raver, *Journal of Land and Public Utility Economics,* III, 343-60.

The cost of laying underground cables would be included in the New York inventory, and omitted from the Chapel Hill inventory. The proportion of wire mileage to instruments would be different because of population density. Many such differences could be enumerated. They bear out the contention that no general index, even for a particular utility industry, can accurately reflect changes in reproduction cost for all utility enterprises.

Finally, it should be noted that apart from the choice of an index, valuations were maintained at a comparatively low level by allowing only part of the indicated increase in construction costs. When the courts began to hold that valuations must reflect fully the indicated rise in costs, commissions gave up the use of the corrective index method of valuation. For a long time, however, commissions succeeded in their policy of allowing only part of the increase in construction costs. This policy was defended on the grounds that reproduction cost was not equivalent to rate making value, for original cost must also be considered; that the rate base must be applied to a future period rather than the current period, so that reproduction cost should be based on expected future prices rather than on current prices; and that under any circumstances utility companies could ask only for normal or reasonable reproduction cost. The valuation methods developed in the war period proceeded on the theory that current prices were unreasonable and abnormal, and need not be fully reflected in the rate base. The corrective index method of valuation applied this theory by allowing a lower index of present value than would be found by using prevailing prices.

CHAPTER VII

VALUATION: THE SPLIT INVENTORY

1. The Split Inventory Method of Valuation

THE SPLIT INVENTORY was the most important of the valuation methods used by commissions and courts in the period from 1916 to 1926. More than any other method, it succeeded in attaining the objects of valuation in this period of high prices: to maintain low rate making values and to avoid the complex valuation procedure. The split inventory method of valuation divides the property to be valued into two parts on the basis of the date of acquisition, and values these parts of the inventory at different unit prices. The property in existence on a given date in the past is generally valued at reproduction cost on that date at current or average unit prices, and all property acquired or constructed thereafter is valued at actual investment. Land is invariably valued at the market price of adjacent lands.[1]

A common form of the split inventory was built up value. In this method of valuation an earlier appraisal generally made before the period of high prices was accepted as basic, and the present value for rate making was found by adding the cost of the property acquired since the earlier valuation. It must be noted that a built up valuation, by utilizing an earlier appraisal, obviated the need for a new valuation proceeding. The basis for a built up valuation was usually an earlier rate base; but when a satisfactory rate base was not available, com-

[1] A prototype of the split inventory, what may be called the classified inventory, has always been accepted as an approved method of valuation. By this method utility property was divided into three classes: land, equipment, and intangibles. Land was invariably valued at its full market value, equipment was generally valued at more than investment but at less than reproduction cost, and intangibles in the form of overhead, etc., were valued at actual cost. There has been considerable discussion of the inconsistency of the classified inventory. See, for example, *Consolidated Gas Co. v. Prendergast* (N. Y.), P. U. R. 1925 B, 798; and *United Fuel Gas Co. v. Public Service Commission* (W. Va.), P. U. R. 1927 A, 707.

missions occasionally used a valuation made for capitalization, sale, or consolidation.[2] If the appraisal was made at the lower prices that prevailed before 1918, such a built up value did not differ in result from the usual split inventory valuation.

To maintain low valuations it was essential to choose a satisfactory date for dividing the inventory. In this, as in other valuation methods of this time, commissions sought a date that might be regarded as representative of normal prices. From 1916 to 1920, the usual split inventory division date was in the period before the United States entered the war. The effect of the choice of this division date was to fix the basic valuation far below current reproduction cost. As the period of high prices continued, commissions chose later division dates. Thus, in New York, where the split inventory method of valuation was used from 1916 to 1926, the commissions used 1914 as the division date in valuations made before 1920, and 1917 and 1918 as the usual division dates in valuations made from 1921 to 1926. Continued high prices thus resulted in higher rate valuations as the division date was advanced into the war period. In many states a uniform division date was generally used in all split inventory valuations, although no uniformity in the choice of a division date can be seen in the different states that used the split inventory method.

The importance of the division date for the inventory is in its relation to unit prices. Many commissions modified the effect of a later division date by the use of average prices in valuing the basic inventory. Five-year averages were frequently used, and longer period averages were occasionally used.[3] The object

[2] See *Re James A. Murray* (Calif.), P. U. R. 1917 C, 521; *Rose v. Mercersburg, Lehmasters & Markes Electric Co.* (Penna.), P. U. R. 1919 F, 714; *Kansas City Railway Co. v. Kansas City* (Mo.), P. U. R. 1918 E, 190; *Re Milton & Milton Junction Telephone Co.* (Wisc.), P. U. R. 1920 C, 110; *Lyons v. Wayne Telephone Co.* (N. Y.), P. U. R. 1921 A, 385; *Re Indiana Bell Telephone Co.*, P. U. R. 1922 E, 46; *Re Chesapeake & Potomac Telephone Co.* (W. Va.), P. U. R. 1921 B, 97.

[3] *Re Illinois Northern Utilities Co.*, P. U. R. 1920 D, 979; *Re Utah Gas & Coke Co.*, P. U. R. 1920 C, 854; *Re Northwestern Bell Telephone Co.* (Minn.), P. U. R. 1922 C, 762.

in using average prices, particularly when the division date was later than 1917, was to maintain low basic valuations while complying with the rule that the prices of the time of valuation must be given consideration. The fundamental purpose of commissions in using the split inventory was to maintain low rate making values, and this was done by eliminating or minimizing high current prices in the basic and in the supplementary valuations.

After hesitant use in 1916, the split inventory method came into common use by 1918, although it was less important at this time than reproduction cost valuation at average unit prices.[4] The great stimulus to the increased use of the split inventory was the decision of the New York Supreme Court in the Brooklyn Borough Gas case, in 1918. This was the most important early split inventory valuation considered by a court, and it had the added prestige of the approval of Chief Justice Hughes, then referee for the New York Supreme Court. The Brooklyn Borough Gas Co. had applied to the court for an order restraining the enforcement of rates prescribed by statute which the company alleged to be confiscatory. The utility company requested a reproduction cost valuation at average prices of 1912 to 1916. The commission had used a built up valuation with 1914 as the division date. In approving the commission's valuation, Mr. Hughes said (P. U. R. 1918 F, 348):

When the value of a plant has been properly determined by the regulating authority, and suitable allowance is made for the investment in subsequent additions, it is manifestly proper to calculate the fair return upon this basis, . . . and there is no reason why there should be substituted for the official appraisal a hypothetical estimate of reproduction cost under abnormal conditions reaching an amount vastly in excess of investment. I conclude that the Commission's appraisal plus an allowance for investment in subsequent additions as shown by the plaintiff's books, affords in this case a proper basis for calculating the fair return to which the plaintiff is entitled.

[4] The split inventory was used before July, 1918, in California, District of Columbia, Illinois, Indiana, Maryland, Missouri, New Hampshire, New Jersey, New York, Ohio, Oregon, and Wisconsin.

The opinion was widely cited, and because of the authority of Mr. Hughes carried great weight with courts and commissions. In particular, the refusal to allow a reproduction cost valuation at five-year average unit prices induced many commissions to change from this method of valuation to the split inventory.

2. THE SPLIT INVENTORY IN NEW YORK

The Public Service Commissions of the first and second districts of New York were among the first to make extensive use of the split inventory method of valuation.[5] As early as 1916 the commission of the first district valued the Newtown Gas Co. by increasing a basic 1914 appraisal by the estimated additional investment (P. U. R. 1916 D, 825), and later in that year the same commission valued the New York Edison Co. on a 1913 split inventory basis, the earlier property being valued at 1913 prices and the latter property at actual investment cost (P. U. R. 1917 A, 364). In upstate New York, the commission of the second district began the use of the split inventory early in 1918, when the Lockport Electric Co. was valued at reproduction cost of 1912, with additions from 1913 to 1916 valued at actual cost (P. U. R. 1918 C, 675). Thereafter, until 1926, the commissions of the first and second districts were definitely committed to the split inventory method of valuation.

Until 1920, the split inventory valuations were accepted without question in New York. In that year the policy of the commission of the second district was tested in the state Supreme Court. In the Mt. Vernon Water case, decided in 1920, the court approved a valuation of the referee in which a corrected appraisal of 1913 was built up by allowing the actual cost of additional investment from the division date to the time of

[5] Throughout this period there were two commissions in New York state. The commission of the first district had jurisdiction in New York City, the commission of the second district in the rest of the state. The policy of these commissions was precisely the same, and because the continuance of this policy was dependent on the approval of the state and federal courts, there is no need to consider their rate cases separately. At present there is only one Public Service Commission in New York. Some of the duties of the earlier commission of the first district are now performed by the Transit Commission of the City of New York.

the new valuation. As in other split inventory valuations, the full appreciation in the market value of land was included in the rate base. In his opinion, Judge Tompkins quoted at length from the Brooklyn Gas case, and emphasized that "this method of arriving at the present value of the plaintiff's property was approved by Judge Hughes" (P. U. R. 1920 D, 520). In 1920 and 1921, the New York Commissions continued to use the split inventory method, generally in the form of built up valuations.[6] The court decisions of 1920 and 1921 that induced other states to abandon the split inventory method of valuation did not affect the policy of the New York Commissions.[7]

An unfavorable decision of the state Supreme Court in the Iroquois Gas case (P. U. R. 1921 B, 485), however, resulted in a modification of the valuation policy of the New York Commissions to the extent of advancing the inventory division date to 1917, when the higher prices of the preceding year could have some effect on the rate making value. The later division date was used in the Utica Gas & Electric case, in which the basic inventory was valued at reproduction cost in 1917, with additions valued at actual cost. "[The basic] valuation . . . midway between 1914 and 1920," said the commission, "reflects the increased war costs of the period. The additions allowed since 1916 reflect the further increases in costs up to the present time" (P. U. R. 1922 A, 149). The commission of the first district adopted the same division date, 1917, in its valuation of the Long Island Gas Co. In denying the applicability of the Iroquois decision, the commission emphasized that its valuation method was in close agreement with that of Chief Justice Hughes in the Brooklyn Borough Gas case (P. U. R. 1922 B, 19).

[6] *Re Glen Cove Telephone Co.*, P. U. R. 1920 D, 529; *Lyons v. Wayne Telephone Co.*, P. U. R. 1921 A, 285; *Re Kingston Gas & Electric Co.*, P. U. R. 1921 B, 76; *Re Southern New York Power & Railway Corp.*, P. U. R. 1921 D, 135.

[7] See the decisions of the New Jersey Supreme Court in the Elizabethtown case, P. U. R. 1920 F, 1001; the Missouri Federal District Court in the St. Joseph case, P. U. R. 1921 A, 540; the District of Columbia Court of Appeals in the Potomac case, P. U. R. 1922 B, 684. In these cases the courts rejected the split inventory, despite the argument of commissions that the method had the approval of Chief Justice Hughes.

Even this modification of the split inventory method of valuation in New York to bring it into closer conformity to the present value rule was not sufficient to satisfy the courts. In the New York State Railways case (P. U. R. 1922 E, 675) the state Supreme Court, and in the New York Telephone case (P. U. R. 1925 A, 491) the Federal District Court held that split inventory valuations were not in accord with the law. Thereafter, the split inventory method was used only in isolated instances in New York in which recent valuations at postwar prices were built up to give present value. This was done in the Peekskill Electric case in which a 1922 valuation was increased by the cost of subsequent additions (P. U. R. 1925 D, 593), and in another Brooklyn Borough Gas case in which a reproduction cost valuation of 1923 was increased by the investment in additions since the basic valuation (P. U. R. 1927 A, 200).

3. The Split Inventory in Wisconsin

The Wisconsin Commission was the strongest advocate of the split inventory method of valuation. Before the war this commission had used reproduction cost at average unit prices. In 1917 the commission abandoned reproduction cost and adopted the split inventory method of valuation. In that year in valuing the Racine Water Co. for municipal purchase, the commission used a 1914 split inventory, the basic property being valued at a five-year average of the prices of materials with partial recognition of the upward trend of labor costs (P. U. R. 1917 D, 277). The commission did not use the split inventory again until 1918 when it valued the Milwaukee electric system at a 1914 split inventory with the basic property appraised at ten-year average prices (P. U. R. 1918 E, 1). Later in the same year, the commission made a built up valuation of the Green Bay Water Co. by taking an appraisal of 1916 as basic and adding to it the cost of subsequent additions (P. U. R. 1918 F, 59).

By 1918, therefore, the split inventory method of valuation had become the accepted policy of the Wisconsin Commission. When a valuation of 1916 or earlier was available, the commission built it up; otherwise, a new 1914 split inventory valuation was made.[8] The commission made frequent use of tentative and temporary valuations. Where such valuations were built up for use in rate proceedings, it was expressly stipulated that they could not be used in later proceedings as evidence of fair value.[9] There was no pretense that valuations fixed in this informal manner represented fair present value with accuracy. They were regarded as an expedient for simplifying valuation procedure in an abnormal period. For this purpose built up valuations were ideal, for they could be completed quickly and economically from previous appraisals and from records of recent investment.

While other commissions were returning to current reproduction cost valuations after 1921, the Wisconsin Commission continued to use the split inventory and defended the method as conforming to the rate making rule. The split inventory, the commission held, gave due consideration to prevailing prices (P. U. R. 1922 C, 829); and it was fairer in the long run to the utility companies and to consumers (P. U. R. 1922 A, 259). Nevertheless, the policy of the commission did not go unchallenged by the utility companies. Until 1925 the state Supreme Court upheld the commission's valuation method. When, however, the federal courts held that the split inventory did not give adequate consideration to the present value of utility property, the state court reversed its position and the commission changed its valuation policy.

The favorable attitude of the state Supreme Court is apparent from its decisions in various split inventory cases. In

[8] For built up valuations, see *Re Twin City Telephone Co.*, 22 Wisc. R. C. R., 229; *Re Portage American Gas Co.*, 22 Wisc. R. C. R., 275; *Re Wisconsin Traction, Light, Heat & Power Co.*, P. U. R. 1919 B, 224; *Re Wood County Telephone Co.*, P. U. R. 1919 F, 226; *Re Rockford & Interurban Railway Co.*, P. U. R. 1920 C, 1010; *Milwaukee v. Milwaukee Gas Light Co.*, P. U. R. 1920 F, 833; *Re Beloit Water, Gas & Electric Co.*, P. U. R. 1921 A, 299; *Re Rose Milling Co.*, P. U. R. 1922 A, 587; *Re Wisconsin Telephone Co.*, P. U. R. 1922 B, 553; *Re City of LaCrosse*, P. U. R. 1924 A, 586.

[9] *Re Eastern Wisconsin Electric Co.*, P. U. R. 1919 F, 640; *Re Elkhart Lake Light & Power Co.*, P. U. R. 1920 A, 345; *Re Milton & Milton Junction Telephone Co.*, P. U. R. 1920 C, 110; *Re Wisconsin Telephone Co.*, P. U. R. 1920 C, 116; *Re Commonwealth Co.*, P. U. R. 1923 A, 689.

upholding a 1912 split inventory valuation in the Waukesha case, the court stressed the compulsory nature of the utility business and the consequent need to protect the investment rather than the reproduction cost of utility property. "Before the jurisdiction of the court can be successfully invoked," said Judge Rosenberry, "it must appear that the property of the plaintiff is being taken, not that it is deprived of the benefit of market fluctuations in the value of materials and labor" (P. U. R. 1923 C, 339). The court refused to consider objections to the split inventory method as such, holding that the ultimate test must be the valuation found rather than the method used. "The constitutional rights of a utility are not invaded by the pursuit of a wrong method of valuation," the court said. "It is not its method that is to be reviewed, but the result reached by the Commission" (P. U. R. 1922 B, 113). While upholding the split inventory, the state Supreme Court nevertheless emphasized that because of the constitutional issue, the judgment of the federal courts would be decisive.

In 1925 a split inventory valuation of the Ashland Water Co. was set aside as confiscatory by the Federal District Court in Wisconsin. The commission had valued the property of the utility company on a 1916 split inventory basis, with ten-year average prices appreciated by 15 per cent applied to the basic inventory, and additions after the division date valued at investment cost. The federal court held it was a denial of the present value rule to appraise the basic inventory at prices prevailing eight years before the valuation, and that it was also repugnant to this rule to value later additions at investment instead of reproduction cost (P. U. R. 1926 B, 292). The state Supreme Court accepted the decision as binding and on a rehearing of the Waukesha case reversed its previous ruling (P. U. R. 1927 B, 545). Under the circumstances, the Wisconsin Commission abandoned the split inventory method of valuation. In the Wisconsin Telephone case, 1927, the commission recognized that rate making value must be "substantially based on present day prices" (P. U. R. 1928 B, 434).

4. THE VALUATION OF THE RAILROADS

In carrying out the provisions of the Valuation Act of 1913 and the Transportation Act of 1920, the Interstate Commerce Commission used the split inventory. The Valuation Act required the commission to determine the value of the property of the railroads, giving consideration to the elements of value recognized by law. Specifically, the commission was required to determine the original cost, the reproduction cost new, the reproduction cost less depreciation, the value of carrier lands, the original and present cost of acquiring the lands, and such other values or elements of value that the commission might find. The act did not specify the purpose for which the values were to be fixed, but it was expected that they would be useful in rate proceedings (75 I. C. C. 1).

The commission experienced great difficulty in determining original cost, for a good deal of railroad property was acquired through gifts, aids, and donations, and it was uncertain how such property should be included in the original cost. Even for comparatively recent property the precise original cost could not be determined with accuracy because of the diversity of railroad accounting methods prior to 1907. The commission therefore contented itself with stating the original cost of such property as it could determine, and giving a probable maximum original cost for the property of the carrier as a whole.

The greatest importance was assumed by the reproduction cost less depreciation estimates. The inventories upon which these appraisals were based were made by the commission's engineers assisted by the carriers. The inventories were taken as of June 30, of the years 1914 to 1919, nearly half of the inventories being as of June 30, 1916. The unit prices were secured from returns made by the railroads. They were requested to report the prices paid for materials in the two largest purchases of each year from 1910 to 1914. For materials that fluctuated considerably in value, prices were taken from the four largest purchases of each year from 1905 to 1914. Labor costs were taken from actual wage rates paid in railroad construction at quarterly intervals from 1910 to 1914 (75 I. C. C. 35).

Although the inventories were taken as of different dates, the unit prices applied were the five- and ten-year averages to June 30, 1914, despite the protest that the use of quantities as of 1915 and later years in connection with unit prices as of 1914 did not give the value of the property on the inventory date (75 I. C. C. 192). The rising prices of 1915 to 1919 were a strong factor in inducing the commission to apply prewar unit costs uniformly for all carriers. Depreciation was estimated on a straight line basis. The railroad lands were valued at the average market price per acre of similar adjoining or adjacent land. Any special value that the lands might have for railroad purposes was taken into account. The present cost and the original cost of acquiring the lands were not determined by the commission, and an amendment to the Valuation Act relieved it of this duty.[10] The railroads were valued as going concerns, so that no separate allowance was made for this or for other intangible elements of value. The railroads objected to the valuations on several grounds, particularly because no detailed analysis was made of the value of each item of property. Although this may not have been necessary under the Valuation Act, it would have been wiser to meet the wishes of the roads in this matter.[11]

The Transportation Act of 1920 made it mandatory for the commission to find a single sum value as a basis for determining fair return, and for other purposes. This value, as of the inventory date, was fixed at reproduction cost less depreciation, to which was added the present value of land, and a further corrective percentage, generally 5 to 10 per cent, to allow for elements not included in the commission's valuation. This additional percentage provided the flexibility that recognized qualitative differences in the economic position of the carriers, differences not revealed in physical valuations. To find

[10] The land valuation policy followed the rule of the Minnesota rate cases, 230 U. S. 352. For the commission's views, see 75 I. C. C. 168, 464; 84 I. C. C. 28.

[11] See H. B. Vanderblue, *Railroad Valuation by the Interstate Commerce Commission.* For the commission's view, see 75 I. C. C. 443, 445; for the carriers' view, see the *Petition of the National Conference on Valuation,* 84 I. C. C. 9.

the final value, the commission called for reports of additions and betterments since the inventory date (75 I. C. C. 140). These additions were valued at actual cost, so that the final values were determined by the split inventory method. A minority of the commission held that the valuations on this basis were not in accord with the law, and cited the rulings of the Supreme Court requiring recognition of present prices in rate making valuations.

In 1927 the commission's valuation policy was taken to the courts. The St. Louis & O'Fallon Railroad had been valued on a 1914 split inventory basis, with later additions valued at actual cost, and land given its present value. The Federal District Court sustained the commission's contention that even at the railroad's own valuation it had earned a fair return after the recapture of excess income (P. U. R. 1928 A, 740). On appeal to the Supreme Court, the lower court was reversed, and the commission's valuation was set aside for failure to consider all the elements of value prescribed by law (P. U. R. 1929 C, 161). The decision leaves the railroad valuation question unsettled, although it is not at present urgent, for it is doubtful whether many railroads could earn a fair return on a valuation higher than that fixed by the commission. It should also be noted that the sharp decline in prices since 1929 may have brought current reproduction cost of the railroads very close, if not quite equal, to the commission's split inventory valuations.

5. THE SUPREME COURT ON THE SPLIT INVENTORY

The rise and fall of the split inventory followed closely the changing attitude of the courts. In 1918 the favorable decision of the New York Supreme Court in the Brooklyn Borough Gas case led to wider use of the split inventory. In 1921 unfavorable decisions in New Jersey, Missouri, and the District of Columbia, led to its abandonment in these and in other states. The ultimate decision on the use of the split inventory was made, of course, by the federal courts, and their attitude was generally unfavorable to valuation methods in which reproduction cost at current prices was not given dominant consideration.[12] However, until the Supreme Court passed upon the split inventory it could not be said with finality whether or not this method of valuation was in accord with the law.

The attitude of the Supreme Court toward the split inventory has been one of hesitation, and despite the O'Fallon decision, is still somewhat in doubt. The first split inventory valuation that reached the court, the Galveston case, has already been discussed as a corrective index valuation. The fair value of the utility company's property was determined by the Federal District Court of Texas on a 1915 split inventory basis, with unit prices of 1915 increased by one-third applied to the 1915 inventory and with later additions valued at actual cost (P. U. R. 1921 D, 547). On appeal to the Supreme Court, the valuation of the District Court was approved. Justice Brandeis, for the court, emphasized that the valuation was not on the basis of prudent investment, and in fact exceeded the actual cost of construction (P. U. R. 1922 D, 159).

In May, 1923, the Supreme Court set aside the Missouri Commission's built up valuation of the Southwestern Bell Telephone Co. When the telephone industry was returned to private management after the war, the Missouri Commission reduced the rates of the Southwestern Bell company. No valuation was made of the property of the telephone company, except that a 1913 appraisal of the St. Louis exchange, and early appraisals of two other exchanges, were built up to give present value. Although approved by the state courts, the valuation was rejected by the Supreme Court. A majority held that the rates were confiscatory because they did not provide a fair return on a valuation reflecting higher prevailing prices. Justice Brandeis and Justice Holmes held that the valuation was unfair because it was less than actual prudent investment. The case is an excellent illustration of the misuse of the split inventory. The company had little property constructed at high war prices,

[12] The federal courts set aside split inventory valuations in *Van Wert Gas Light Co. v. Public Utilities Commission* (Ohio), P. U. R. 1924 C, 722; and in *Chesapeake & Potomac Telephone Co. v. Public Service Commission* (Md.), P. U. R. 1925 D, 407.

the basic appraisal was made at the low prices of 1913, and the valuation was hastily and carelessly made from a part of the property of the company (P. U. R. 1923 C, 193).

Less than three weeks later, June, 1923, the Supreme Court decided two split inventory cases, sustaining the valuation in one and setting it aside in the other. In 1920 the West Virginia Commission valued the Bluefield Water Co. on a 1915 split inventory basis. The valuation was approved by the state courts, but was set aside on appeal to the Supreme Court. Justice Butler for the court held that insufficient consideration was given to the higher construction costs of 1920, the time when the valuation was made. Justice Brandeis concurred in the judgment for the reasons he stated in the Southwestern Bell Telephone case (P. U. R. 1923 D, 11). Seemingly the same problem was presented in the Georgia case. The commission valued the utility's property on a 1914 split inventory basis. The Federal District Court sustained the valuation (P. U. R. 1920 C, 744), and it was affirmed by the Supreme Court. Justice Brandeis, for the court, emphasized that although the basic valuation was as of 1914, the company was allowed the increase in the value of its land, and its full investment at high prices although the reproduction cost of these additions was then less than their investment cost. The court said that "the refusal of the commission and of the lower court to hold that, for rate making purposes, the physical properties of a utility must be valued at the replacement cost less depreciation was clearly correct" (P. U. R. 1923 D, 1). While there is great similarity in the valuation methods in the Bluefield and Georgia cases, the results were admittedly not the same. For the Georgia company the split inventory valuation was in excess of investment, for the Bluefield company it was not.

When the O'Fallon case came before the Supreme Court there was general agreement among those writing on the question that the court would distinguish railroads from other utilities, and would sustain the valuation of the Interstate Commerce Commission.[13] In its decision of May, 1929, the court made

[13] See the papers by J. C. Bonbright and E. C. Goddard, *Harvard Law Review*, XLI, 564, 593.

no such distinction, and set aside the 1914 split inventory valuation of the railroad on the ground that it gave insufficient consideration to the prices prevailing at the time of the inquiry. Justice Brandeis and Justice Stone in their dissenting opinions pointed out that "the general method pursued by the commission in reaching its conclusion closely resembles that approved by the court" in the Georgia case (P. U. R. 1929 B, 219). In considering the O'Fallon decision in the light of other split inventory cases, one must conclude that it is not the split inventory method that is unconstitutional, but that when improperly used the split inventory will result in a confiscatory valuation. What is proper and what is improper use of the split inventory is still uncertain.

6. An Appraisal of the Split Inventory

As with other valuation methods in the war and postwar period, commissions sought to attain two objects by the use of the split inventory: to fix low valuations, and to avoid complex valuation procedure. The first object was realized to some extent in the use of average prices and corrective indices; but they were open to the objection that revaluations had to be made at intervals in the same manner as the original valuation. With the split inventory, on the other hand, after the first valuation the rate base could be determined from the accounts showing additional investment. As the Washington Supreme Court said, the split inventory contemplated "but one valuation proceeding. All subsequent proceedings are rate making proceedings" (P. U. R. 1927 C, 781). Not infrequently split inventory valuations were built up three and four times.

Another advantage of the split inventory as a means of valuation in this period of high prices arose from the distinction it made between early property constructed at low cost, and later property constructed at high cost. The use of average prices was certain to antagonize either the utilities or the consumers. If the property was acquired largely before the war, consumers felt that the utility company was profiting unjustly when average unit prices for a period including the war years were used.

On the other hand, if much of the property was acquired in the period of high prices, the utility company was aggrieved. It could argue that its investment, say in 1919, was made at prices 100 per cent above the 1913 level because a commission had ordered it to expand its facilities. To value this property in the very year it was acquired at average prices only two-thirds of the actual cost seemed, quite understandably, a form of confiscation. The split inventory avoided this difficulty by differentiating property constructed at high prices from property constructed at low prices. In its valuation, it neither confiscated recently acquired property nor offered a bounty on older property.

It must be emphasized that no method of valuation can permanently maintain low valuations. The ultimate purpose of the new valuation methods should have been to provide a means for gradually changing the level of the rate base from prewar prices to postwar prices. The split inventory was well suited to achieve this purpose. As additional investment was made, greater weight was given in split inventory valuations to the postwar price level, and as property was depreciated or retired less weight was given to the prewar price level. Because this took place gradually, the transition from prewar prices to postwar prices would have occurred slowly but with certainty. Eventually, when the whole of the prewar property would have been retired, the rate base would have been permanently established at the prudent investment of the utility company. Throughout the period of transition, the property rights of utilities would have been protected, for by the nature of the split inventory method of valuation, the minimum rate base at any time would have been equal to or in excess of the actual investment in the property.

It has been said that the split inventory valuations could not be in compliance with the rule of *Smyth v. Ames*. For most commissions it may be said that they used the split inventory by virtue of a liberal interpretation of the valuation rule. Where the inventory was divided in the period of high prices, say in 1918, a considerable part of the property was valued at more than actual cost, and land was always appraised at the market value of adjoining lands. In this manner, considerable influence was exerted by high current prices on every part of the split inventory valuation. The fact that the courts, including the Supreme Court, at times approved this method of valuation would indicate that when properly applied the split inventory can be fair to utility companies and consumers. Fundamentally, the split inventory gave whatever result commissions wished it to give. It is not the method but its application in some cases that was open to objection. It is not too much to say that if commissions had taken a broader view of the situation after 1923, it might have been possible to modify the split inventory valuations sufficiently to make them satisfactory to the courts, and even to the utility companies.

The desirability of the split inventory as a method for transforming valuation from a prewar basis in which reproduction cost at prewar prices predominated to a postwar basis in which prudent investment at postwar prices predominated must depend on the economic merits of prudent investment valuation. It cannot be emphasized too strongly that differences between reproduction cost value and prudent investment value have their origin in changing price levels. With fairly stable prices there are no great economic advantages in one rather than the other method of valuation. With fluctuating prices, the economic merits of either method are hopelessly confused with class interests and conflicts. But the administrative advantages of prudent investment valuation in providing an economical and flexible method of adjusting rates to changing conditions of cost are so great as to warrant a preference for this method of valuation. The service the split inventory could have rendered the community was to provide a means for gradually establishing the prudent investment as the measure of the rate base.

CHAPTER VIII

THE FAIR RATE OF RETURN

1. The Problem of Rising Interest Rates

THERE ARE TWO important aspects of the problem of fair rate of return. The first is the factors that should be given consideration if a constitutionally fair rate of return is to be determined. On this question there has, on the whole, been little disagreement. While differences in emphasis on one factor or another arose occasionally, courts, commissions, and utility companies have succeeded in arriving at an acceptable method of determining fair rate of return. However, in the period of high interest rates during and after the war, controversy arose as to the weight to be given to these abnormally high interest rates in the fair rate of return. On the second aspect of the problem of fair rate of return—the base on which a fair rate must be allowed—greater difficulties have been encountered. The courts have long held that the fair value of the property used and useful in providing utility services must be the basis for the fair return. In *Smyth v. Ames*, the Supreme Court held that the utility company's securities cannot be given sole consideration, for this apparent value may be fictitious and unfair (169 U. S. 544). Nevertheless, some economists and commissions believe that the fair return should be related to the capital charges of a utility enterprise, if these charges for interest and dividends have been prudently incurred.[1]

Because there was fundamental agreement on the factors affecting fair rate of return, commissions developed the custom, before the war, of allowing a standard rate of return that was regarded as compensatory for utility companies of average efficiency.[2] This standard rate of return was not the same in all

---

[1] See the previous discussions on rate of return, Chap. II, section 3, and Chap. III, section 4, above.

[2] See C. O. Ruggles, "Problems of Utility Regulation and Fair Return," *Journal of Political Economy*, XXXII, 543; J. H. Bickley, "A Fair Return for Public

states, although it was generally fixed at 6 or 7 per cent until 1918. Because the interest rate was the dominant factor in determining the rate of return, the standard rates that had long been regarded as fair became unacceptable to utility companies in the period of high interest rates from 1918 to 1924. Commissions were therefore faced with the problem of considering again the fair rate of return that would be just in each case. The question was a difficult one for commissions at this time, for they were already heavily burdened with the duties of frequent revaluation and they could not easily assume the additional duty of determining at frequent intervals fair rates of return for many utility companies. Further, commissions were eager to maintain utility rates at as low a level as possible in this period of high prices and interest rates. To accomplish this it was necessary not only to minimize fair value by giving little weight to current high prices, but also to minimize fair rate of return by giving little weight to current high interest rates.

With the reopening of the question of fair rate of return, it was inevitable that some commissions would attempt to apply the fair rate of return to the stockholders' proprietorship rather than to the fair value of the property of the utility company. This method, which requires the commission to allow interest on bonds and dividends on preferred stock as capital charges, and then to determine a fair rate of return to be applied to the outstanding common stock, had long been in use in Massachusetts. During the period of high interest rates, the method was also used in several other states. Obviously, the common stock basis for return minimized the effect of high interest rates, for any increase in the fair rate of return would apply only to the common stockholders' interest in the utility property and not to the entire rate base. This method of determining return has seemed so desirable that proposals have recently been made to modify the rate making rule to permit its use.[3] Even com-

Utilities," *Journal of Land and Public Utility Economics*, III, 61; H. D. Dozier, "Reasonable Rate of Return in Public Utility Cases," *Journal of Land and Public Utility Economics*, IV, 235.

[3] D. R. Richberg, "A Permanent Basis for Rate Regulation," *Yale Law Journal*, XXXI, 273. See also, Chap. X, section 3, below.

missions that did not use the common stock basis for return succeeded in continuing relatively low fair rates of return by using the average rate paid on capital invested in the enterprise, much of it represented by bonds and preferred stock receiving low prewar rates of interest and dividend, as evidence of the fair rate of return.

Although some commissions would have preferred to replace the present method of determining fair rate of return by a new method requiring a fixed return based on the actual cost of acquiring the capital prudently invested in the enterprise, no attempt was made to regulate rates by this principle. It was advocated by Justice Brandeis and Justice Holmes in a concurring opinion in the Southwestern Bell Telephone case, but a majority of the Supreme Court held that it was too far a departure from the rate making rule (P. U. R. 1923 C, 193). Nevertheless, the desirability of this method of determining return was considered by commissions in the period of high interest rates, and more recently the use of this method has been proposed in the Bauer plan submitted to a New York legislative commission as a satisfactory solution of the rate making problem.[4]

2. A TEMPORARY DEFICIENCY OF RETURN

The rise in interest rates, and the even greater rise in construction costs after 1917, caused many commissions to seek means to prevent the tremendous increase in the return to public utility companies that would result from applying a higher rate of return to a much higher rate making value. In part this was accomplished by the use of new methods of valuation that succeeded in maintaining the rate base below reproduction cost at current prices. Less spectacular, but nevertheless quite important, were the methods used by commissions to prevent the fair rate of return from rising commensurately with higher prevailing interest rates.

[4] The proposal for a fixed rate of return as a solution to part of the rate making problem is discussed more fully in Chap X, section 3, below.

Yield on Fifteen High Grade Utility Bonds, 1913 to 1926*

Year	Yield Per Cent	Year	Yield Per Cent
1913....................	4.94	1920..................	6.73
1914....................	4.87	1921..................	6.56
1915....................	4.88	1922..................	5.46
1916....................	4.79	1923..................	5.41
1917....................	5.09	1924..................	5.22
1918....................	5.76	1925..................	5.06
1919....................	5.84	1926..................	4.90

Standard Statistics Base Book. It should be noted that the yield on lower grade utility securities fluctuated more sharply.

As early as 1917, some commissions stated the view that not only must utility companies not expect to receive higher rates of return, but that even the normal return need not be allowed on the theory that utilities should share the burdens of war. When the Utah Commission allowed a return of only 5.4 per cent, the case was taken to the state Supreme Court where the commission's ruling was upheld. The court said that while utility companies are ordinarily entitled to a fair and reasonable return, such a return could not be assured when conditions were abnormal. At such a time, "every individual and every enterprise must bear his or its share of the burden incident to the great conflict" (P. U. R. 1918 F, 377).

A rate of return below that prevailing before the war was justified by several commissions as a temporary condition that would correct itself in time. Even before the war it was recognized that fluctuations in return were part of the risk of conducting a utility business (P. U. R. 1915 C, 525; P. U. R. 1915 F, 747). The commissions of New York, as well as of other states, permitted rates that yielded unusually low returns to continue in force for some time with the comment that ordinary inequalities in return for passing periods could not be regarded as confiscation (P. U. R. 1919 D, 76). However, the New York Commissions could not continue to neglect fixing rate schedules to yield fair rates of return. In the Queens Gas case (P. U. R. 1921 A, 530), and in the Kings Gas case (P. U. R. 1921 A, 737), the Federal District Court held that periods of more than a year were sufficient for testing the confiscatory nature of rates, and that inadequate rates must be revised, even in an abnormal period. In response to this decision, the New York Commissions allowed a return of 8 per cent on their valuations in 1921 and for some years after.

Whatever tendency there was to fix rates that yielded an unusually low return was checked by the unequivocal decisions of the courts. The Federal District Court of Ohio held in the Toledo electric case, that a utility company could not be expected to operate at a loss on the theory that it should sacrifice some of its income in the emergency of war (P. U. R. 1919 C, 230). Even more explicit was the decision of the Supreme Court in the Lincoln Gas case. The court noted that "annual returns upon capital and enterprise the world over have materially increased, so that what would have been a proper return for capital invested in gas plants and similar public utilities a few years ago furnishes no safe criterion for the present or the future" (250 U. S. 256). In view of this decision, commissions could not continue the practice of allowing a rate of return below that prevailing before the war.

3. A NORMAL RATE OF RETURN

A method frequently used by commissions to minimize the fair rate of return was to allow the prewar standard rate on the theory that a fair rate of return could be defined as a normal rate of return. This was analogous to the use of normal value as a measure of fair value in determining the rate base. Many commissions made use of the doctrine of normal rate of return on occasion. In Indiana and in Illinois it was the policy of the commissions to use normal rates of return in their rate proceedings from 1918 to 1926. By this means higher interest rates were not permitted to bring about a corresponding rise in fair rates of return.

Early in 1918 the Illinois Commission rejected the contention that utility companies petitioning for higher rates should be content with returns much less than were ordinarily adequate and reasonable (P. U. R. 1918 D, 919). Instead, the commission decided that the prewar standard rate of return should be continued as the normal rate of return. Throughout 1915 and 1916, the standard rate had been between 7 and 7.5 per cent, and until 1918 the utility companies were content to accept this as a fair rate of return. In 1918 the Rockford Traction Co. demanded a return of 10 per cent on its rate making value on the ground that higher interest rates justified this rate of return. Nevertheless, the commission allowed a return of only 7 per cent (P. U. R. 1918 F, 840). The commision was affirmed in its policy of maintaining the normal rate of return when the state Supreme Court held that a return of 7 per cent was reasonable in the important Springfield Gas case (P. U. R. 1920 C, 640).

In 1920, when interest rates reached their highest level, the Illinois Commission announced that it would give consideration to this condition in determining fair rate of return. In fact, however, it did not modify its policy on the rate of return to any noticeable extent, for although it allowed rates of return slightly in excess of 7 per cent in some instances, there were other instances in which a return of only 6 per cent was allowed.[5] In general, it may be said that the Illinois Commission was successful in maintaining its prewar standard return of 7 to 7.5 per cent throughout the period of high interest rates; and with the decline of interest rates in 1922, the utility companies in that state seem to have relaxed their claim to higher rates of return.

The Indiana Commission also made extensive use of the policy of allowing only a normal rate of return in the period of high interest rates. The standard rate of return in Indiana before the war was 7 per cent. In 1917 and 1918, during the war, the Indiana Commission held that utility companies could not be assured the fair normal rate of return, but must be content with returns of 5 to 6 per cent.[6] In 1919, with the war over,

[5] For a return in excess of 7 per cent, but not exceeding 8 per cent, see *Re Chicago Railways Co.*, P. U. R. 1921 A, 466; *Re Sterling Water Co.*, P. U. R. 1921 A, 801; *Re Metropolitan West Side Elevated Railway Co.*, P. U. R. 1921 B, 229. For a 6 per cent return, see *Re Interstate Water Co.*, P. U. R. 1922 E, 246; *Re Rockford Gas Light & Coke Co.*, P. U. R. 1922 E, 756.

[6] The Indiana Commission held that utility companies must share the burdens of war in *Re Noblesville Heat, Light & Power Co.*, P. U. R. 1918 B, 766; *Re LaPorte Gas & Electric Co.*, P. U. R. 1918 F, 666; *Re Indianapolis Water Co.*,

this rule was modified to the extent of resuming the 7 per cent standard rate of return.[7] It is interesting to note that in a series of rate cases for the Indiana Bell Telephone Co., in this period, the commission never allowed a return as high as 7 per cent, because poor service, inefficient management, and increased expenses from unwise mergers had resulted in rates regarded as excessively high (P. U. R. 1922 C, 348; P. U. R. 1926 C, 785).

The policy of the Indiana Commission of allowing a normal rate of return was approved by the state Supreme Court. In 1920, the Columbus Gas Co. asked that its rates be modified to allow a return of 8 per cent, citing as justification the prevailing high interest rates. The commission fixed rates intended to yield a return of 7 per cent (P. U. R. 1920 F, 606). When the case was taken to the state courts it was found, in fact, that the commission's rates yielded a return of only 6.58 per cent. Nevertheless, the court ruled that the utility company had failed to show that this rate of return, although less than 7 per cent, was confiscatory (P. U. R. 1922 E, 602). After this decision, the utility companies in Indiana showed little inclination to contest the fairness of the standard rate of return; and with the decline in interest rates in 1922, it would have been difficult to convince the commission and the state courts of the inadequacy of a 7 per cent return.

4. INTEREST, DIVIDENDS, AND THE RATE OF RETURN

In 1918, when the financial condition of many utility companies became precarious, President Wilson and Secretary McAdoo called attention to the necessity of allowing utilities a return sufficient to meet their corporate financial obligations. At the same time the War Finance Corporation ruled that no securities could be issued by any utility company that did not meet its outstanding obligations. In response to these views

---

P. U. R. 1919 A, 448; *Re Interstate Public Service Co.*, P. U. R. 1919 A, 686; *Re Indianapolis Traction & Terminal Co.*, P. U. R. 1919 B, 152; *Re Sullivan City Water Co.*, P. U. R. 1919 B, 539.

[7] *Re Reddington Telephone Co.*, P. U. R. 1919 F, 141; *Re Gary Street Railway Co.*, P. U. R. 1920 A, 191; *Re Union Telephone Co.*, P. U. R. 1920 F, 391; *Re Indianapolis Street Railway Co.*, P. U. R. 1921 B, 133.

many commissions ruled that corporate financial needs would measure the minimum return that would be allowed. In 1919, the Maryland Commission suggested that the doctrine of corporate needs replace the rule of *Smyth v. Ames* in rate making, and added that in several cases it had been governed "by the existing corporate requirements" in determining the fair return (P. U. R. 1920 A, 1). Despite the suggestion of the Maryland Commission, the doctrine of corporate needs was not widely used as a measure of fair return, although the commissions of New York, Masachusetts, and some other states, were guided to some extent by interest and dividend rates on utility securities in determining the fair rate of return.

Theoretically, the doctrine of corporate financial needs would require that the return allowed to utility companies should be sufficient to meet interest on bonds and dividends on preferred stock at the rates called for in these securities, and to permit that rate of dividends on common stock that would maintain the market value of the stock at par. Thus the return to utility companies would be precisely enough to permit continued operation and to induce sufficient further investment, at par, to provide for necessary expansion. Actually, commissions determined the fair value by whatever valuation method they used, and applied to this a fair rate of return determined on the basis of the interest rate on outstanding bonds and the dividend rate on outstanding stock. The corporate financial needs of the utility company in this manner indirectly affected the fair rate of return.[8]

In Massachusetts, it had been customary, even before the war, to consider interest and dividend requirements in determining the fair rate of return. In allowing the Bay State Railways a return of 6 per cent in 1916, the commission held that this would be sufficient, because half of the investment consisted of bonds with average annual charges of 4.7 per cent, leaving 7.3 per cent as the return to the stockholders (P. U. R. 1916 F, 221). Later in 1916 the Massachusetts Commission allowed a re-

---

[8] The place of the doctrine of corporate needs in wartime rate making policy is discussed in Chap. IV, section 2, above.

turn of 6.2 per cent in the New Haven Railroad rate case emphasizing that with much of the capital borrowed at low interest rates, this would permit an adequate return to stockholders (P. U. R. 1917 B, 904). During the war, the commission began the practice of allowing a return sufficient to meet interest requirements on bonds, and to pay dividends of 6 per cent to stockholders (P. U. R. 1918 B, 231; P. U. R. 1918 C, 515). After the war higher returns were allowed to stockholders, although the commission continued to determine the rate of return with reference to charges for interest on outstanding bonds.

The New York Commissions also made extensive use of the financial cost method of determining the fair rate of return. In 1915 the commission of the second district allowed a return of 6.75 per cent, because it was sufficient for the payment of 6 per cent to bondholders and 8 per cent to stockholders (P. U. R. 1916 B, 940). In 1916 the commission of the first district held that a return of 7 per cent was compensatory if the rate on outstanding bonds was only 5 per cent (P. U. R. 1916 D, 825). During the war the New York Commissions were inclined to maintain rather low rates of return on the theory that utility companies should bear their share of the burdens of war. The commission of the second district went so far as to say that "neither the appeal of President Wilson nor the ruling of the War Finance Corporation had in view the maintenance in all cases of normal profits" (P. U. R. 1918 D, 918). Nevertheless, it was recognized by the commission that ordinarily corporate financial needs represented the minimum fair return (P. U. R. 1919 A, 214). When the New York Commissions resumed the use of a standard rate of return of 8 per cent after 1920, this was justified as sufficient in view of the much lower interest rates at which outstanding bonds had been issued (P. U. R. 1920 D, 257).

It should be noted that many commissions rejected the doctrine that corporate financial needs are a measure of the fair return. The Illinois Commission said that the principle was not in harmony with the rulings of the courts, and that in determining the fair return it would not be guided by the sums needed to pay interest and dividends on outstanding securities (P. U. R. 1920 B, 726). The commission preferred to maintain the normal rate of return that it had used in the period before the sharp rise in interest rates. The Wisconsin Commission similarly held that the fair return must be determined on the basis of the fair value, and not by the amount required for dividends (P. U. R. 1920 F, 833). The greatest opposition to the consideration of interest and dividend requirements in determining the fair rate of return came, as would be expected, from the courts.

5. The Supreme Court on Fair Rate of Return

The rise in interest rates was not so great as the rise in construction costs, and courts were for that reason less inclined to permit a deviation from the accepted method of determining fair rate of return. In the influential Elizabethtown case, Judge Swayze of the New Jersey Supreme Court held that because of the rise in interest rates and the greater risks of conducting a business, an 8 per cent return, although fair in 1913, was not compensatory in 1919 (P. U. R. 1920 F, 1003). The courts were particularly opposed to the practice of determining the rate of return with reference to the interest and dividend requirements on outstanding securities. The Virginia Supreme Court of Appeals said on this point: "That for which the utility company is entitled to 'just compensation' is the use of its property appropriated to the public benefit, and the value of that use is founded upon the fair value of the property so used, and not upon the amount of stock it has issued or the debts it may owe" (P. U. R. 1922 C, 172). On occasion, however, state courts did hold that the financial structure of a utility could be considered in determining the fair rate of return (P. U. R. 1922 C, 258).

Despite the higher cost of acquiring new capital, rates of return between 7 and 8 per cent were generally approved by the lower federal courts (P. U. R. 1920 F, 328; P. U. R. 1925 C, 744). There is no indication, however, that they approved the determination of fair return on the basis of interest and dividend requirements. The question of fair return in this period received more critical consideration in the Supreme Court. Before the war the court had regarded a return of 6 per cent as compensatory. In the Lincoln Gas case, 1919, the court decided that a return of 6 per cent at that time was confiscatory. In explaining this departure from its previous standard, the court emphasized that the continued rise in interest rates and profits in all industries everywhere had made the compensatory rate of return in the utility industries correspondingly higher, so that the pre-war standard return of 6 per cent could no longer be regarded as adequate under the rate making rule (250 U. S. 268).

In subsequent cases, the views of the Supreme Court were more definitely established. In the Galveston case, the fair rate of return was overshadowed by the more controversial question of valuation. The Federal District Court had approved a split inventory valuation on which a return of 8 per cent was allowed. It was agreed that for the preceding eighteen months the rate schedule had not yielded sufficient net revenue to provide a return of 8 per cent on the fair value. The District Court held that the prospect of a rise in receipts and a fall in operating expenses justified the continuation of the prescribed rate with the expectation that it would soon yield a compensatory return. The Supreme Court sustained the decision. Justice Brandeis, for the court, emphasized the abnormality of the period and the favorable prospect of earning the return of 8 per cent in the near future (P. U. R. 1922 D, 159).

The cleavage in the Supreme Court on the question of fair rate of return became apparent in the Southwestern Bell Telephone case. The court was unanimous in holding the rate schedules of the Missouri Commission confiscatory. A majority of the court held that this was because the rates did not yield a fair rate of return on the reproduction cost of the property. Justice McReynolds, for the court, said that the indicated return of 5.33 per cent was wholly inadequate considering prevailing interest rates. Justice Brandeis and Justice Holmes concurred in the decision, but based their conclusion on the principle that compensatory rates should yield enough to meet the actual financial charges on the capital prudently invested in the enterprise. "Where the financing has been proper, the cost to the utility of the capital required to construct, equip and operate its plant, should measure the rate of return which the Constitution guarantees opportunity to earn" (P. U. R. 1923 C, 214). The financial cost theory of return thus received the approval of part, although rejected by a majority, of the Supreme Court.

In the Georgia case, the Supreme Court held that a return of 7.25 per cent on a 1914 split inventory valuation was compensatory. Although the court was divided on the question of fair value, there seems to have been no difference of opinion on the fairness of the rate of return (P. U. R. 1923 D, 1). In the Bluefield case, a 1915 split inventory valuation on which a return of 6 per cent had been allowed was set aside as confiscatory. Justice Butler, for the court, emphasized that a return of 6 per cent was inadequate to induce continued investment of capital in the utility industry. Justice Brandeis concurred in the result, but reaffirmed the views he had stated in the Southwestern Bell Telephone case (P. U. R. 1923 D, 11). In 1924, in the Dayton-Goose Creek Railway case, the Supreme Court was called on to consider the rate of return under the Transportation Act of 1920. The Interstate Commerce Commission had set 6 per cent as the basic return for determining recapturable excess earnings. The court did not pass on the adequacy of the 6 per cent return, however, because the earnings of the railway, after deducting recaptured earnings, were sufficient to yield a return of 8 per cent on the fair value (263 U. S. 456).

The Indianapolis Water case again brought a division of the Supreme Court on the fair rate of return. The rates fixed for the Indianapolis Water Co. were intended to yield a return of 7 per cent on reproduction cost at ten-year average prices. The Federal District Court found the rate base to be confiscatory, and the return sufficient to yield only 5 per cent on a proper valuation. On appeal, the Supreme Court ruled that a reasonable rate of return was not less than 7 per cent, and that the commission's rates did not yield that return on a fair value of the company's property. Justice Brandeis and Justice Stone dissented, holding that there was no reason for regarding a return of less than 7 per cent necessarily confiscatory (P. U. R. 1927 A,

15). It is worth noting that while the case was pending, the Indiana Commission in another rate proceeding for the same company fixed a fair rate of return at 6.5 per cent, citing as evidence of the fairness of this return the yield of only 5.45 per cent on the utility securities held in the depreciation reserve account of the company (P. U. R. 1925 C, 431).

6. SUMMARY AND CONCLUSIONS

There is a striking resemblance between the methods developed by commissions to maintain low rate making values and the methods developed to maintain low rates of return. In determining fair rate of return, as in valuation, commissions sought a normal level that would not be a hardship to consumers or utilities. The use of the prewar normal rate of return was justified as reasonable in a period of abnormally and temporarily high interest rates. Later developments proved that commissions were right in their contention that the high interest rates of 1920 and 1921 were temporary, for by 1922 the yield on high grade utility bonds was only one-half per cent higher than in 1913.

Aside from the doctrine of a normal rate of return, no great innovation took place in this aspect of rate making during the period of high prices and high interest rates. Justice Brandeis called attention to the desirability of determining the rate of return on the basis of actual charges required to meet interest and dividend payments on outstanding securities, but no commission made use of this method of determining the rate of return. In Massachusetts and in New York, and to a lesser extent in Virginia, the fair rate of return fixed by the commissions was applied to the common stockholders' proprietorship rather than to the fair value, the low interest charges on bonds being regarded as a capital expense. But the method did not have the approval of the courts, and was never widely used. The doctrine of corporate needs, which resembles the capital cost method of determining return, was an expedient used only for a short time in 1917 and 1918.

Perhaps the most surprising result of the controversy on the fair rate of return was the great rise in the minimum rate of return regarded as compensatory by the courts. Until 1916 the Supreme Court had regarded a return of 6 per cent as compensatory under ordinary conditions. At that time the standard rate of return allowed by commissions in most states was not less than 6 per cent, and more often 7 per cent. It is not quite certain why the Supreme Court was so lenient in its attitude toward fair rate of return in the period before the war. There was a theory advanced that a rate might be unreasonably low without being confiscatory, but the Supreme Court never recognized this distinction. Whatever the reason, it is certain that after the war the court was less inclined to accept a rate of return slightly below the prevailing rate. In the Indianapolis Water case, in 1926, the Supreme Court held that a return of 7 per cent was the minimum that could be regarded as compensatory, although the yield on high grade utility bonds in that year was actually below the 1913 level. It will be shown in the following chapter that during the period of prosperity at the end of the 1920's the Supreme Court raised the minimum return that it regarded as fair to more than 7 per cent, although in the recent great depression it permitted much greater reductions in the fair rate of return than it had allowed even during the war period.

CHAPTER IX

RATE MAKING IN PROSPERITY AND DEPRESSION

1. The Valuation Question in Prosperity

With the repeated rejection of new methods of determining fair value and fair rate of return, nearly all commissions, after 1926, resumed the use of the accepted rate making procedure: preparation of an inventory, the determination of unit prices, dominant or exclusive consideration of reproduction cost in valuation, and the application of a fair rate of return to the fair value. There were a few commissions, particularly the California Commission, that attempted to maintain valuation at investment cost, but the courts were firm in rejecting their valuation methods.[1] For most commissions the immediate objective of rate making in the prosperous years of 1928 and 1929 was to prevent the complete exclusion of investment cost from consideration in valuation, and to prevent the high profits in competitive industry in these years from raising the accepted rate of return far above the 6 or 7 per cent that had long been regarded as fair.

Although the Supreme Court had repeatedly cited the valuation principles of *Smyth v. Ames* requiring consideration of investment cost, it nevertheless seemed to identify fair value with reproduction cost at current prices. There was protest from commissions in 1928 and 1929 that the practical exclusion of investment cost from consideration was a denial of the valuation principles that the Supreme Court had always upheld. "The tendency has been and is to state that cost of reproduction is not the sole evidence of value, but to make it the sole evidence of value by

---

[1] See, for example, *Re Southern California Telephone Co.*, P. U. R. 1929 E, 610; *Re Los Angeles Gas & Electric Corp.*, P. U. R. 1931 A, 132; *Re San Joaquin Light & Power Corp.*, P. U. R. 1923 D, 310. The Federal District Court in *Pacific Gas & Electric Co. v. California Railroad Commission* held that refusal to consider reproduction cost is a denial of due process, 13 P. U. R., New Series, 520. In the Southern California Telephone case, the commission gave consideration to all factors in determining the fair rate making value, 14 P. U. R., N. S., 252.

ignoring other evidences of value," the Indiana Commission observed. "This commission does not believe that cost of reproduction should be excluded as evidence of value of utility property, nor does it believe that cost of reproduction should control to the exclusion of other evidences of value" (P. U. R. 1928 C, 296). Even the courts were cognizant of this tendency among them to pay lip service to all factors affecting value while, in fact, making reproduction cost the measure of fair value. The Federal District Court in New York rejected the statement of a special master on valuation, emphasizing that reproduction cost is not the legal equivalent of fair value, as the master held, but only evidence of value (P. U. R. 1930 B, 33).

Most commissions, although they disagreed with the Supreme Court on the desirability of valuation at reproduction cost, held that they were bound by law to accept it as the dominant if not the exclusive factor in determining fair value. It would have been impossible for commissions to hold otherwise, for most courts were firm in their view that the Supreme Court had decided that reproduction cost at current prices was equivalent to fair value. The Federal District Court in Massachusetts, where the commission was inclined to give great weight to investment, presented the prevailing attitude toward reproduction cost in the Worcester Electric case. "As the decisions of the Supreme Court now stand," said the court, "it seems clear that federal courts must determine the question of confiscation by reference to present value, and that, in cases like the present, the reproduction value less depreciation is a fair measure of that value, and in the absence of special controlling circumstances, it may be considered as the dominant element" (P. U. R. 1929 B, 1). For this reason commissions valued utility property at reproduction cost, despite a frequently expressed preference for investment cost as the measure of the rate base.

2. Fair Rate of Return in Prosperity

Although commissions had reluctantly accepted reproduction cost less depreciation as the dominant element in valuation, they were not willing to allow materially higher rates of return in the prosperous years of 1928 and 1929 than had been allowed previously. The yield on high grade utility bonds in 1928 and 1929 was approximately the same as in 1926 and 1927, and somewhat lower than in 1924 and 1925. Unquestionably, profits in industrial enterprises were considerably higher in 1928 and 1929 than they had been in earlier years of the decade. However, commissions had no reason to believe that industrial profits must be given greater weight than the current cost of acquiring new utility capital in determining the fair rate of return.

YIELD ON FIFTEEN HIGH GRADE UTILITY BONDS, 1923 TO 1930*

Year	Yield Per Cent	Year	Yield Per Cent
1923	5.41	1927	4.78
1924	5.22	1928	4.68
1925	5.06	1929	4.80
1926	4.90	1930	4.65

*Standard Statistics Base Book. It should be noted that the yield on lower grade utility securities fluctuated more sharply.

Throughout 1928 and 1929, there were states in which the rate of return was maintained at a moderate level, that is, at 7 per cent or less. In Maine, the practice was to allow a return of not less than 6 per cent nor more than 7 per cent. In Illinois, it was also customary to permit a return between 6 and 7 per cent, although for a time in 1929 a return of 7.5 per cent was allowed in some cases. In Pennsylvania and in many other states commissions prescribed a uniform return of 7 per cent. There were several important states, however, in which the usual rate of return was from 7 to 8 per cent. Included in this group were such well regulated states as New York, California, and Missouri. It may be said, therefore, that the prevailing rate of return in 1928 and 1929 was from 6 to 8 per cent, with a return of 7 per cent most common.[2]

[2] For a return of less than 7 per cent, see Re Camden & Rockland Water Co. (Me.), P. U. R. 1929 E, 325; Re Illinois Bell Telephone Co. (Ill.), P. U. R. 1928 E, 279. For a return of 7 per cent, see Knoxville v. South Pittsburgh Water Co. (Penna.), P. U. R. 1928 B, 204; Re Madison Railways Co. (Wisc.), P. U. R. 1928 C, 842; Re Southern Indiana Telephone & Telegraph Co. (Ind.), P. U. R. 1929 E, 641. For a return of more than 7 per cent, see Re Iroquois Gas Corp.

The views of the federal courts were, on the whole, favorable to maintaining a standard return of 6 to 7 per cent in 1928 and 1929. In the Greencastle Water case, the Federal District Court in Indiana approved a return of 6.5 per cent (P. U. R. 1929 D, 287). In the Fort Worth Gas case, the Federal District Court in Texas accepted a report of the master who found that a return of 7 per cent would be reasonable (P. U. R. 1930 C, 203). In the Cambridge Electric case, the Federal District Court in Massachusetts refused to grant an injunction restraining the enforcement of rates that yielded a return of less than 8 per cent. "We are not at present satisfied," the court said, "that a return of less than 8 per cent would *ipso facto* be confiscatory" (P. U. R. 1928 E, 258). Commissions were seemingly justified in holding that the prevailing fair rate of return, approximately 7 per cent, was acceptable to the courts as adequate under the constitutional provision protecting utility property.

Under the circumstances, the Supreme Court's decision in the Baltimore street railways case was entirely unexpected. The Maryland Commission in 1928 established fares for the United Railways intended to yield a return of 6.26 per cent. The company urged that a return of less than 8 per cent would not be fair, although it stated that it would be content with a return of approximately 7.5 per cent. In deciding on a return of 6.26 per cent the commission was influenced by the fact that no street railway in the larger cities of the East was earning much more than 6 per cent (P. U. R. 1928 C, 604). A majority of the Maryland Court of Appeals twice approved the commission's rate order (P. U. R. 1928 D, 141; P. U. R. 1929 B, 467).

Despite the able report of the commission and the previous decisions in the state courts of Maryland, the Supreme Court set aside the rate order of the commission. Justice Sutherland, for the court, said (P. U. R. 1930 A, 228, 232):

What is a fair return . . . cannot be settled by invoking decisions of this court made years ago based upon conditions radically different from those which prevail today. The problem is one to be

(N. Y.), P. U. R. 1930 D, 30; *Re Los Angeles Gas & Electric Corp.* (Calif.), P. U. R. 1929 C, 3; *Re Laclede Gas Light Co.* (Mo.), P. U. R. 1929 C, 561.

tested primarily by present day conditions. . . . In this view of the matter, a return of 6.26 per cent is clearly inadequate. In the light of recent decisions of this court and other federal decisions, it is not certain that rates securing a return of 7.5 per cent or even 8 per cent on the value of the property would not be necessary to avoid confiscation. But this we need not decide, since the company itself sought from the commission a rate which it appears would produce a return of about 7.44 per cent, at the same time insisting that such return fell short of being adequate.

Justice Brandeis, in a dissenting opinion, said that a net return of 6.26 per cent on the present value of a street railway enjoying a monopoly in a large and prosperous city would seem to be sufficiently compensatory.

The effect of the decision was to induce the courts to require higher rates of return. The Circuit Court of Appeals held that the rates fixed for the Elizabethtown, N. J., Water Co., yielding a return of less than 7.25 per cent, were confiscatory (P. U. R. 1930 E, 375), although water utilities in that state had never been allowed so high a return. If the depression had not set in at this time, it is likely that the prevailing rate of return would have been raised to a minimum of 8 per cent.

3. THE DOCTRINE OF REASONABLE WORTH

The severe depression after 1929 brought with it an insistent demand for lower utility rates. With reduced operating expenses, construction costs, and interest rates, it would have been possible to bring about some decline in utility rates while allowing to utility companies a liberally fair rate of return on the fair value of their property. What was desired was a decrease in rates beyond this level. Justification for this departure from the rate making rule was found in *Smyth v. Ames,* in the statement recognizing a limitation on a utility's right to a fair return. "What the company is entitled to ask is a fair return upon the value of that which it employs for the public convenience. On the other hand, what the public is entitled to demand is that no more be exacted from it . . . than the services rendered are reasonably worth" (169 U. S. 546).

It was argued by some commissions that with the fall in prices and incomes the value of utility services had declined, and that under the doctrine of reasonable worth rates could be reduced even if they did not provide a fair rate of return on the fair value of the utility company's property. The Maine Commission stated that the determination of reasonable rates involved the financial condition and the ability to pay of those receiving the services. The Wisconsin Commission ruled that even when a general reduction in rates could not be granted, rates should be lowered for rural subscribers, a class that suffered severely from the economic depression. In California, the commission held that a graduated schedule of rates should be established, varying from year to year with the level of prices of the principal crops of the community.[3]

Obviously the doctrine of reasonable worth was not acceptable to the utility companies. Nor were the courts willing to approve extreme application of this doctrine. "No authority has been cited, and we know of none," said the Washington Supreme Court, "to the effect that the value to the consumer, or his ability to pay, is the prime factor which alone will warrant the reduction of a rate affording no more than reasonable compensation." The court added: "Public service companies are not eleemosynary institutions, and they cannot be compelled to devote their property to a public use except upon the well-recognized basis of a fair and reasonable return therefor" (7 P. U. R., N. S., 18, 19).

The decline in commodity prices was also regarded as justifying a considerable reduction in utility rates under the doctrine of reasonable worth. The Tennessee Commission said that with the increased purchasing power of money it was to be expected that a dollar should buy more electricity than it did in 1929 (P. U. R. 1932 E, 386). The Michigan Commission, however, did not regard the decline in commodity prices as necessitating similar reductions in utility rates, pointing out that in the past

[3] *Damariscotta-Newcastle Water Co. v. Itself* (Me.), 12 P. U. R., N. S., 539; *Mergen v. Farmers Telephone Co. of Lancaster* (Wisc.), P. U. R., 1933 B, 420; *Re East Side Canal Co.* (Calif.), 3 P. U. R., N. S., 307.

rates for electricity were falling while commodity prices were rising (P. U. R. 1933 E, 193). The Ohio Commission said on the same question: "Unfortunately, it is impossible for us, under the law, to fix a rate that may depend upon the cost of commodities, except so far as the price levels may affect the value of property used and useful" (P. U. R. 1933 D, 164). Despite these views to the contrary, it was common for commissions to cite the fall in commodity prices as justification for a reduction in utility rates.

Having decided that the lower level of incomes and prices required a reduction in utility rates, many commissions proceeded to bring about this reduction by the use of emergency orders. The method used in Wisconsin was to fix temporary rates that provided a return of approximately 6 per cent on book cost, substantially prudent investment, for the duration of the emergency period, generally one year. The commission recognized that even emergency rate orders must not be confiscatory, but it also held that a return of 5 to 6 per cent on the book value of a utility company could not be regarded as confiscatory in a period of severe depression.[4] In New York, the commission, as provided by law, allowed a return of not less than 5 per cent, usually 6 per cent, on the original cost of the utility's property. Despite this, the lower courts in that state held on several occasions that emergency rate orders based on the statute were unconstitutional. Ultimately, however, these orders were upheld by the New York Court of Appeals.[5]

The great obstacle to the wider use of emergency rate orders was the doubt that existed as to their constitutionality. Unless courts and commissions permitted a temporary deficiency in the fair return, under the doctrine of reasonable worth, it was impossible to use emergency rate orders. There was little hesita-

---

[4] For emergency rate orders in Wisconsin, see *City of Mauston v. Mauston Telephone Co.*, P. U. R. 1933 E, 161; *Gates v. Tigerton Electric Co.*, 1 P. U. R., N. S., 97; *County of Oneida v. Valley Electric Co.*, 1 P. U. R., N. S., 312.

[5] *Re Yonkers Electric Light & Power Co.* (N. Y.), 6 P. U. R., N. S., 132; *Re Bronx Gas & Electric Co.* (N. Y.), 6 P. U. R., N. S., 198. These orders were set aside by the state Supreme Court, but upheld by the Court of Appeals, 14 P. U. R., N. S., 337.

tion among commissions on this point, but the federal courts were quite emphatic in their opposition to any departure, even temporarily, from the rate making rule. In setting aside an order of the Utah Commission, the Federal District Court ruled that confiscatory rates cannot be justified on the ground that they are designed to be temporary (5 P. U. R., N. S., 293). And the Federal District Court in Missouri held that temporary rates are not exempt from the requirement of providing a fair rate of return on the fair value of utility property (6 P. U. R., N. S., 10).

4. CORRECTIVE INDEX VALUATION IN DEPRESSION

The rate making problem in a long depression could not be solved by emergency rate orders effective for a year or less. It was necessary to bring about reductions in rates by showing that the fair rate of return on the fair value of utility property had declined. There was no difficulty in proving this. The authority of the reproduction cost doctrine as a measure of fair value facilitated the process of reducing rates, for it was obvious that with the decline in the prices of materials and the wages of labor, the reproduction cost of utility property had fallen considerably. Some commissions, it seemed, were delighted that the reproduction cost doctrine could at last be applied in favor of the public. In the United Fuel Gas case, 1932, the West Virginia Commission observed (P. U. R. 1932 B, 79):

The reproduction rule has been accepted only after stubborn but respectful resistance on the part of state commissions, very largely for the reason that under it the increasing price levels that followed the outbreak of the World War, and prevailed for more than a decade, resulted in increased charges for utility service. . . . The downward trend of price levels the past few years and the probabilities of a continuation of the curve appear to promise some compensation to the ratepayer for whatever he has suffered from the reproduction theory of valuation during the years of high material and construction costs. It may be that the public and the commissions would abandon the rule now as reluctantly as they have hitherto accepted it.

The decline in reproduction cost endangered the financial stability of those utility companies that had acquired much of their property in the period of high prices. Utilities tried to minimize the reduction in valuations by requesting the use of average prices in reproduction cost estimates. In some instances commissions were inclined to give weight to the higher prices of the 1920's, particularly where actual investment had been undertaken at these prices.[6] Generally, however, commissions preferred to take advantage of lower current prices to bring about large reductions in fair value. It is interesting to note that some of the commissions that opposed the use of average prices at this time had made use of this device in the period of high prices during and after the war.

An interesting aspect of valuation during the depression was the revival of the use of corrective indices. In this valuation method, an earlier rate base or the original cost was corrected by the application of an index number to give present fair value. There were several reasons why commissions preferred to use corrective indices. First, the delay and expense involved in a valuation proceeding would have prevented prompt reduction of rates. Second, because public utility construction had practically ceased, the available unit prices were fictitious, that is, quotations made for the purpose of facilitating a valuation. Under the circumstances, commissions preferred to use an objective index number of prices or construction costs, particularly as the use of a sensitive index number would result in a much lower rate base.

The most commonly used indices were the Bureau of Labor Statistics index number of wholesale prices, the *Engineering News-Record* index number of construction costs, and particular indices prepared for specific valuations. The North Carolina Commission in valuing the Southern Bell Telephone Co. said that the Bureau of Labor Statistics index number of wholesale prices was the best measure of the decrease in the value of utility property since its construction (7 P. U. R., N. S., 21). The New York Commission, on the other hand, held that this

[6] *Re Salem Electric Light Co.* (N. H.), 7 P. U. R., N. S., 550; *Commercial Club of Chambersburg v. Chambersburg Gas Co.* (Penna.), P. U. R. 1933 D, 317; *State ex rel. Oregon-Washington Water Service Co. v. Department of Public Works* (Wash.), 11 P. U. R., N. S., 478.

index number could not be satisfactory because the commodities in the collection were not precisely those used in utility construction, and because wage rates were not included in this index number of prices (P. U. R. 1932 E, 218). The South Carolina Commission expressed a preference for the use of the *Engineering News-Record* index number of construction costs in correcting a book value to find present reproduction cost (P. U. R. 1923 C, 351).

The most elaborate use of a corrective index in valuation during the depression occurred in the Maryland telephone case, in 1933. To avoid the delay and expense of the usual valuation procedure, the company and the commission agreed to the use of a corrective index. A 1923 valuation that had been fixed by a federal court was corrected by a "fair value translator" which was the weighted average of 16 index numbers of prices, wages, and construction costs (1 P. U. R., N. S., 346). The company objected to the fair value that was found in this manner. The Federal District Court held that the commission was wrong in "assuming that an average trend of all prices, whether absolute or weighted, is a true index for the trend of construction costs of the special kind of property" of the telephone company (3 P. U. R., N. S., 241). On appeal to the Supreme Court, the decision that the valuation was not in accord with the requirement of due process was sustained, although admittedly the company had originally agreed to an index number valuation. In a vigorous dissent, Justice Stone said that no evidence in the record disputed the fairness of the valuation, and that it ought not to be set aside merely because index numbers had been used (8 P. U. R., N. S., 433).

5. THE RATE OF RETURN IN DEPRESSION

During the depression, commissions directed much of their attention to reducing the rate of return that was allowed on utility property. The yield on high grade utility bonds—ordinarily the most important factor affecting the rate of return—declined somewhat in 1930 and 1931, but rose sharply in 1932 and 1933. Despite the behavior of the market for utility securities, commissions succeeded in bringing about a considerable reduction in the fair rate of return. Justification was found in the greatly reduced earnings of industrial enterprises. "It hardly seems fair," said the New York Commission, "that every utility should be entitled to at least 6 or 7 per cent upon the fair value of its property in all periods regardless of the burden which a widespread depression places upon all other enterprises." The commission noted that "the United States Supreme Court recognized an increased rate of return when conditions were prosperous. Will it accept the corollary of this proposition and fix a low rate of return as the limit of confiscation in periods of depression?" (P. U. R. 1933 B, 64).

YIELD ON FIFTEEN HIGH GRADE UTILITY BONDS, 1929 TO 1936*

Year	Yield Per Cent	Year	Yield Per Cent
1929...................	4.80	1933...................	5.18
1930...................	4.65	1934...................	4.31
1931...................	4.60	1935...................	4.61
1932...................	5.36	1936...................	4.01

*Standard Statistics Base Book. It should be noted that the yield on lower grade utility securities fluctuated more sharply.

A similar attitude toward the relation of the rate of return to industrial profits in depression was manifested by other commissions. In Washington a return of 4.64 per cent was held to be sufficient in a period of severe depression (P. U. R. 1933 E, 289). The Oregon Commission ruled that the general decline in corporate earnings from 1931 to 1933 justified a considerable reduction in the fair rate of return to public utilities (8 P. U. R., N.S., 87). The Indiana Commission took testimony of bankers and business men that a return of 5 per cent to utility companies was adequate in view of the reduced earnings in other enterprises (P. U. R. 1932 A, 16). In a discussion of utility rates during the economic emergency, the Pennsylvania Commission unanimously resolved that so long as depression continued, a return of 6 per cent on the fair value of utility property would be adequate and reasonable (3 P. U. R., N. S., 123).

On the whole, the courts were sympathetic to this point of

view. When it is recalled that in 1930 the Supreme Court held that a return of 6.26 per cent was confiscatory, and that a return of 7.5 or 8 per cent might be necessary, the tolerant attitude of the courts toward reduction of the rate of return is remarkable. The Virginia Supreme Court of Appeals held that a return of 4.98 per cent during depression was not confiscatory (7 P. U. R., N. S., 53). The Federal District Court in Illinois said that with depressed industrial conditions it would not be warranted in finding a probable return of 5.17 per cent inadequate (P. U. R. 1933 B, 145). Most important, the Supreme Court gave an affirmative answer to the question of the New York Commission whether it would approve lower rates of return in depression. In the Dayton electric case, the court upheld an order of the Ohio Commission that yielded a return of 6.5 per cent. Justice Cardozo, for the court, said: "In view of business conditions, of which we take judicial notice, the rate allowed was adequate. Whether a lower rate could be upheld is a question not before us" (3 P. U. R., N. S., 294).

On the other hand, there was considerable opposition to reduction of the rate of return to public utilities merely because of the fall in industrial profits. In the West Palm Beach Water case, a special master for the Federal District Court in Florida said that there was no authority for determining the rate of return on utility investments by the standards of return in other lines of business (P. U. R. 1930 A, 222). Several commissions held that utility companies had not been permitted to make fabulous profits during the war and in the great boom of the 1920's, and for that reason ought to be protected from the destructive effects of depression.[7]

Several commissions revived the use of the common stock basis for return. It was the practice of the New York Commission, during the depression, to set rates that yielded 6 per cent on the stated value of the utility's common stock after meeting interest charges (2 P. U. R., N. S., 307). In Massachusetts, the

---

[7] *Re Birmingham Gas Co.* (Ala.), P. U. R. 1923 B, 241; *Re Public Utility Rates and Service* (N. C.), P. U. R. 1932 E, 321; *Re Arkansas Power & Light Co.* (Ark.), 5 P. U. R., N. S., 161.

commission continued to establish rates that provided fair dividends to common stockholders—generally 6 per cent of the average price at which the stock had been issued (5 P. U. R. N. S., 333). In Wisconsin, the commission fixed rates sufficient to permit all expenses to be met and to provide a dividend of 6 per cent on the common stock, with a moderate amount of earnings available to increase the surplus. Such a return, the commission said, was liberal in an economic depression of grave proportions (P. U. R. 1932 D, 272). Where the common stock basis for return was used, except in Massachusetts, it was regarded as an emergency device rather than as an accepted method of determining the fair rate of return.

Despite these innovations, most commissions continued to fix rates based on the principle of allowing a fair rate of return on the fair value of utility property. Quite properly, this fair rate of return was held to be somewhat lower in depression than it had been in prosperity. Thus, while 8 per cent was a commonly accepted rate of return in 1929, the maximum that was generally allowed in 1931 was 7 per cent. In 1932 and 1933, a standard return of 6 per cent was almost uniform throughout the country, although some commissions allowed even less. This low standard rate of return was continued in many states all during the period of depression and early recovery. In several states, the fair rate of return was raised to 6.5 or 7 per cent in 1935 and 1936. Thus, at the end of 1936, the fair rate of return was again approaching the standard level of the early part of the 1920's.[8]

Although some federal courts were reluctant to approve rates of return below 7 per cent, even in 1933,[9] many state and federal courts approved returns of 6 per cent or less.[10] The Su-

---

[8] A return of 7 per cent was commonly allowed in 1931 in Colorado, Indiana, Michigan, Missouri, Ohio, Pennsylvania, Washington, and West Virginia. A return of 6 per cent was allowed in 1932 or later in Arizona, Arkansas, Connecticut, Indiana, Louisiana, Maryland, Massachusetts, Minnesota, New Jersey, New York, North Dakota, Ohio, Pennsylvania, Rhode Island, Texas, and Wisconsin.

[9] Federal courts held that a return of 8 per cent or more was necessary in Nevada, P. U. R. 1933 B, 191; in Kansas, P. U. R. 1933 B, 225; and in Texas, 7 P. U. R., N. S., 178.

[10] State courts approved a return of 6 per cent or less in North Dakota, 12

preme Court, although more cautious in its rulings, agreed that lower rates of return must be accepted by public utilities. While a return of 4.53 per cent to the West Ohio Gas Co. from 1928 to 1931 was held to be so low as to be confiscatory (6 P. U. R., N. S., 449), a return probably not in excess of 6 per cent was approved in the Illinois Bell Telephone case. In this case the Supreme Court used dividend payments as evidence of non-confiscation. "The financial history of the Illinois Company repels the suggestion that during all these years it was suffering from confiscatory rates," the court observed. "During this period appellee paid the interest on its debt and 8 per cent dividends on its stock" (3 P. U. R., N. S., 337).

6. SUMMARY AND CONCLUSIONS

The period from 1929 to 1936 brought no major modification in the methods of determining fair value and fair rate of return, although it emphasized again the difficulties of rate making in periods of large and sudden changes in prices and interest rates. The fall in prices from 1929 to 1933, accompanied by a depression of unparalleled severity, necessitated frequent revision of the fair rate making value of utility property. It was obviously impossible for commissions to make new valuations for many utility companies at relatively short intervals. Not only did commissions lack the facilities required for making numerous valuations under the usual procedure, but these valuations, because of rapidly changing prices, would have been inapplicable under the present value rule by the time they were completed. The use of index numbers was a logical method of maintaining the present value basis for rate making, although it necessarily involved abandoning the usual valuation procedure. It was undeniable that some types of index number, notably the Bureau of Labor Statistics index number of wholesale prices, were not satisfactory measures of current construction costs for public util-

---

P. U. R., N. S., 353; in Ohio, 15 P. U. R., N. S., 443; in Oregon, 13 P. U. R., N. S., 337; in Pennsylvania, 14 P. U. R., N. S., 73; and in Texas, 11 P. U. R., N. S., 283. Federal courts approved a return of 6 per cent or less in Indiana, P. U. R. 1933 B, 222; in Illinois, P. U. R. 1933 E, 301; and in Georgia, 2 P. U. R., N. S., 234.

ity property. If the necessity or the desirability of the present value rule is admitted, however, it is difficult to see how the use of index numbers, despite their shortcomings, can be avoided in periods of rapidly changing prices.

The fluctuations that were permitted in the fair return from 1929 to 1936 were much greater than would ordinarily have been expected. Although rates of return far above the prewar level were allowed in the war and postwar period, these higher rates of return were justified to some extent by the higher interest rates required to attract additional utility capital. The great fluctuations in the accepted fair rate of return in the periods of prosperity and depression from 1929 to 1936 were not accompanied by corresponding changes in the interest and dividend rates for new utility capital. The courts, and to a lesser extent commissions, seem to have adopted a new rule, that the fair rate of return must follow industrial profits. The danger to the stability and growth of the utility industries in the adoption of a rule increasing the variability of return must not be overlooked. The managers of utility enterprises should not be distracted from their task of providing efficient and economical utility service at a fair profit by the prospect of speculative gains or losses that a variable return would bring about in periods of prosperity or depression. Above all, it is not desirable that the financial stability of utility enterprises, involving the possible interruption of service, should be endangered in every depression by a policy of permitting widely variable returns. Finally, it must not be overlooked that sharp fluctuations in fair value and in fair rate of return are a cause of protracted investigation and expensive litigation, the ultimate cost of which must be borne by consumers and investors.

CHAPTER X

A PROPOSED SOLUTION

1. Necessary Changes in Rate Making

THE FREQUENCY with which public utility commissions sought new methods of determining fair value and fair rate of return during the periods of unstable prices and interest rates shows clearly that the rate making rule has not been entirely satisfactory. Specifically, the objections are that its procedure is unnecessarily complex, and that it does not provide a method of determining fair value and fair rate of return with precision and certainty. The difficulties of rate making in accordance with this rule are great under any circumstances, and they become so intensified during periods of rapidly changing prices and interest rates, that commissions are compelled to ignore the rate making rule in practice. While it may have been necessary in the early days of commission regulation to avoid a rigid rate making formula, the time has come to consider whether the rate making rule may not be wisely modified to permit simplification of rate making procedure and greater certainty in the determination of fair value and fair rate of return.

From the administrative point of view, the principal objection to the rate making rule is that its procedure is slow, expensive, and conducive to litigation. It has been apparent for a long time that the established procedure is an obstacle to efficient regulation of utility rates. The preparation of a long detailed inventory, the determination of fair unit prices, the estimate of observed depreciation, the valuation of overheads and intangibles, the fixing of a fair rate of return: all this is a costly and time consuming process. The preparation of a rate schedule for one large utility company in this manner may cost several hundred thousand dollars and may occupy a commission for months, to the neglect of other important duties. Even with this elaborate procedure there is no assurance that the fair value and the fair rate of return, so laboriously determined by the commission, will be acceptable to the utility company and consumers. There may then follow extended litigation in state and federal courts, while desirable rate changes are held in abeyance. No one will question the desirability of a modified procedure that will reduce delay and expense without denying justice to the producers and consumers of utility services.

In addition to the simplification of procedure, although not unrelated to procedure, it is necessary that a uniform rule for determining fair value and fair rate of return should be adopted. The Supreme Court has frequently said that valuation is not a matter of applying formulas, for valuation must ultimately be a matter of judgment. In fact, it is quite impossible for those concerned with so difficult a problem as rate making to avoid the use of a more or less definite formula. At the urgent request of the utility companies, many state and federal courts have applied a current reproduction cost formula in valuation. On the other hand, commissions have frequently expressed a preference for the use of prudent investment as the exclusive measure of rate making value. The lack of a precise valuation method, which if uniformly applied would meet with the approval of the courts, has encouraged litigation in the hope that some higher or lower valuation would ultimately be established as fair by the courts. Even with the present rate making procedure regulation can be made more effective by a precise and unequivocal statement from the Supreme Court of an acceptable uniform method for determining fair value and fair rate of return.

The twofold objective of a simplified rate making procedure and a uniform method of determining fair value and fair rate of return could be attained if utility companies would accept and the courts would approve the use of prudent investment as the measure of fair value, and either the capital cost or the common stock basis for determining fair rate of return. This desirable rate making policy, if properly administered, can unquestionably be made attractive to the utility companies, and with their consent should not be objectionable to the courts. Before discussing various methods that have been proposed to induce utility companies to accept this modification of rate making procedure, it would be well to consider once more the major objection to the use of prudent investment valuation and to the capital cost or common stock basis for return.

2. PRUDENT INVESTMENT AND CAPITAL COST

The one great objection to prudent investment valuation is that it fails to bring about a precise adjustment of the present cost of providing utility services and the rates at which these services are sold. A rise or fall in the cost of reproducing a utility plant is indicative of a change in the cost of producing utility services. Under the circumstances, if prudent investment is used as the measure of the rate base, utility services will be sold for more or less than their present cost of production. Consumers may then be uneconomically excluded from the use of utility services by the maintenance of rates above the present cost of production, or uneconomically supplied with excessive utility services by the maintenance of rates below the present cost of production. This inequality of price and cost must result in an improper distribution of the productive resources of the community among its various industries.[1] Further, if rates are not adjusted to the present cost of producing utility services, it is possible that under certain conditions an industry may be diverted from a more to a less favorable locality. For if the rate base is measured by investment, the advantage of a community in some field of production may be determined by the price level at which its utilities were constructed and not by industrial factors.[2] These objections to prudent investment valuation may be summarized in the statement that it does not permit rates to respond sufficiently to changing costs of providing utility services.

There is implicit in these objections an erroneous view of the responsiveness of prices to costs under competition, and of the desirability of equality of prices and present costs under changing

[1] For a fuller discussion of the relative merits of reproduction cost and prudent investment, see Chap. III, sections 2 and 3, above.

[2] H. G. Brown, "Railroad Valuation and Rate Regulation," *Journal of Political Economy*, XXXIII, 505.

economic conditions. It must not be overlooked that in competitive industry prices tend to equal costs only in the long run. For short periods, where the time of gestation or the useful life of capital equipment is relatively long, prices may be more or less than present costs of production for a time. In short periods, prices are adjusted by business men to maximize the current income in excess of operating expenses, and only gradually do prices tend to conform to costs. Under changing economic conditions, it is better for a community to have its productive capacity fully utilized or to induce a necessary expansion of its productive capacity, even if this requires a discrepancy between prices and costs. Although it is desirable to have a tendency for prices to equal costs in the long run, it is not essential to have precise equality of prices and costs in the short run.

In fact, prudent investment valuation is more responsive to changing construction costs than is generally believed. Assuming that the property of a representative utility company is retired at a uniform rate, that depreciation is calculated on a straight line basis, and that net investment in the property is constant, it can be shown that the prices of recent years will have considerable weight in a prudent investment valuation. With these assumptions, if the average length of useful life of the property were ten years, 18.2 per cent of the property in a prudent investment valuation would be valued at the prices of the current year, and 72.7 per cent of the property would be valued at the prices of the five most recent years. If the average length of useful life of the property were twenty years, 9.5 per cent of the property would be valued at the prices of the current year, and 42.7 per cent of the property would be valued at the prices of the five most recent years.[3]

If the net investment in utility enterprises is expanding, and obviously it is at a rapid rate, prudent investment valuation is even more responsive to changing construction costs. Let us assume that the property of a representative utility is retired at a

---

[3] If the sinking fund basis for depreciation is used, the influence of recent prices on prudent investment valuation is even greater. For the probable length of life of various types of utility property, see C. E. Grunsky, *Valuation, Depreciation and the Rate Base*, pp. 418-31.

PERCENTAGE OF PROPERTY VALUED AT PRICES OF MOST RECENT YEARS
(Prudent investment, constant net investment)

Most Recent Years	10-Year Average Life	15-Year Average Life	20-Year Average Life	25-Year Average Life
	per cent	per cent	per cent	per cent
1..................	18.2	12.5	9.5	7.7
2..................	34.5	24.2	18.6	15.1
3..................	49.1	35.0	27.1	22.2
4..................	61.8	45.0	35.2	28.9
5..................	72.7	54.2	42.7	35.4
6..................	81.8	62.5	50.0	41.5
7..................	89.1	70.0	56.7	47.4
8..................	94.5	76.7	62.9	52.9
9..................	98.2	82.5	68.6	58.2
10..................	100.0	87.5	73.8	63.1

uniform rate, that depreciation is calculated on a straight line basis, and that the net investment is expanding 5 per cent annually. Then, if the average length of useful life of the property were ten years, 20.9 per cent of the property in a prudent investment valuation would be valued at the prices of the current year, and 77 per cent of the property would be valued at the prices of the five most recent years. If the average length of useful life of the property were twenty years, 12.6 per cent of the property would be valued at the prices of the current year, and 52 per cent of the property would be valued at the prices of the five most recent years.

PERCENTAGE OF PROPERTY VALUED AT PRICES OF MOST RECENT YEARS
(Net investment expands 5 per cent annually)

Most Recent Years	10-Year Average Life	15-Year Average Life	20-Year Average Life	25-Year Average Life
	per cent	per cent	per cent	per cent
1..................	20.9	15.5	12.6	10.9
2..................	38.8	29.2	24.1	20.9
3..................	54.0	41.3	34.4	30.0
4..................	66.6	52.0	43.7	38.3
5..................	77.0	61.4	52.0	45.8
6..................	85.1	69.4	59.4	52.7
7..................	91.4	76.4	66.0	58.9
8..................	95.8	82.2	71.8	64.5
9..................	98.7	87.1	77.0	69.5
10..................	100.0	91.1	81.4	74.0

The use of the actual cost of acquiring utility capital for determining fair rate of return would not permit great responsiveness to changing interest rates. The force of this objection is diminished somewhat by the fact that interest rates, except in extraordinary times, change very slowly. If the fair rate of return were determined by capital cost, it would be changed only as new securities are issued and as old securities are refunded. Because utility bonds are issued for long periods, and common stock is issued for the life of the enterprise, refunding is not likely to have much effect on the fair rate of return, if that rate is determined by capital cost. Nor would the issue of new securities to the extent of 5 per cent annually of the current net investment increase to any great degree the responsiveness of the fair rate of return to changing interest rates.

The common stock basis for return, on the other hand, would show some sensitivity to changes in the current rate at which new capital is acquired. Under this method, interest on bonds and dividends on preferred stock would be allowed as capital expense, and the fair rate of return to common stockholders would be fixed at that rate which would maintain the market value of the common stock at par. As the issue of common stock represents a significant part of the utility capital, considerable influence on the fair rate of return would be exerted by the market rate for new utility capital.

3. The New York Rate Making Proposals

The importance of modifying the present methods of utility rate making has been repeatedly noted by commissions in many states. There has been a disposition on the part of legislatures to take the view that because the federal courts have jurisdiction over the fairness of rates under the Fourteenth Amendment to the Constitution, nothing can be done by legislation to remedy the evils of the prevailing methods of rate making. In New York, however, an attempt was made in 1929 to find some solution for the rate making problem by a commission chosen by the legislature and by President Roosevelt, then governor of the state. The plans for modifying the present methods of determining fair value and fair rate of return that were considered by this commission offer the hope that a satisfactory way out of our rate making difficulties can be found.

The chairman of the New York Public Service Commission, Mr. William A. Prendergast, presented an ingenious plan for the use of corrective indices and a modified split inventory as a means of simplifying valuation procedure (*Report*, p. 95; *Hearings*, pp. 402-17).[4] The plan provided that by negotiation and agreement with the utility companies, the public service commission should fix the fair value of utility property by the following method. A 1917 inventory of all property other than land would be made basic and valued at book cost. At intervals of two years the commission, with the consent of the utility company, would transform the book value of the basic property to present value by the use of appropriate index numbers. All property other than land acquired after 1917 would be valued at actual book cost, although it might be necessary to apply index numbers to some items in this category. Land would be included in the rate base at its present value, and allowances would be made for working capital and going value at each biennial valuation. Depreciation would be determined by inspection, although if excessive depreciation reserves were accumulated some allowance might be made for this in the valuation.

The Prendergast plan is open to many objections. Under this plan utility companies could require the use of the usual valuation procedure if it suited their purposes. The calculation of accurate index numbers would be almost as difficult as the determination of unit prices in reproduction cost valuation. And the commission would still be required to make frequent revaluations—that is, at the two-year intervals provided by the plan.

A majority of the commission, appointees of the legislature, in the report of its counsel, Colonel William J. Donovan, rec-

---

[4] The evidence taken; by the commission, and the reports of a majority and minority of the commission and its counsel, are contained in four volumes constituting *The Report and Hearings of the Commission on Revision of the Public Service Commissions Law* (hereafter referred to as *Report* or *Hearings*).

ommended the stabilization of the rate base by means of a contract between the utility companies and the public service commission. A present fair value agreed upon by a utility company and the commission would be embodied in a contract for a period of ten or fifteen years. Additions to this basic property after the contract date would be valued at actual cost, and retirements and depreciation would be deducted as shown by the accounts (*Report*, pp. 100-4). After the initial valuation, the rate base under the Donovan plan would be determined from the accounts.

The plan has considerable merit, although it is open to the objection that the delay and expense of the initial valuation would have to be incurred periodically with the renewal of contracts. It was estimated that valuation for all utilities in New York would cost $30 million, and would require four years. If the contract period were only ten years, "a large part of this extremely short period will be taken up with the initial valuation of the property, leaving only a scant few years of grace before the whole miserable and time consuming process of valuation must be done over again."[5]

Dr. John Bauer proposed a valuation plan that met with the approval of a minority, the Roosevelt appointees, on the New York legislative commission. He proposed that legislation be enacted directing the public service commission to determine the present value of utility property according to the rule of *Smyth v. Ames*. Property acquired after the enactment of the law would be valued at actual cost. Depreciation and retirements would be deducted as shown by the reserve accounts of the company. In this manner, the rate base would ultimately be fixed at the prudent investment in the property (*Report*, pp. 392-400). Doubt was expressed of the constitutionality of the Bauer plan. It was generally agreed that the legislature could prescribe by statute the terms on which future investment in utility enterprises would be compensated. It was uncertain whether the legislature could by statute fix the present value of

[5] From a statement of Dr. James C. Bonbright, a member of the legislative commission, quoted in *The New York Times*, April 2, 1930.

existing utility property. For this reason the Bauer plan provided as an alternative that companies could enter into a contract with the public service commission for the use of this method of valuation for a period of approximately twenty-five years.

The New York legislative commission also considered plans for modifying the present method of determining fair rate of return. A majority of the commission proposed in the Donovan plan that a fair rate of return be determined for the existing property, that this fair rate of return be specified as compensatory in a contract for a period of ten or fifteen years, and that the return on additional property should be fixed at the actual cost of acquiring new capital through the securities issued for the purpose (*Report*, pp. 104-8). A minority of the commission proposed in the Bauer plan that a fair rate of return on existing property be determined by the public service commission, this fair rate of return not to be subject to fluctuation in the future because of changing interest rates or the profitability of business. The rate of return on additional property would be determined by the actual cost of acquiring new capital through the securities issued for the purpose, new issues of common stock under this plan calling for a specified return (*Report*, pp. 415-17). The Bauer plan also called for the establishment of an equalization reserve of excessive earnings that would be available to meet deficits in the return of a given year.

4. A Solution to the Problem

The importance of modifying the rate making rule to simplify procedure and to give greater certainty to rate making value is generally admitted. It is worth noting that every plan submitted to the New York legislative commission made provision for the use of prudent investment as a measure of rate making value for all property acquired after the initial valuation. No solution to the rate making problem is possible unless it offers some means for replacing the present complex and unsatisfactory method of rate making with a simpler method under which utility companies would be given a fair return on the prudent investment in their property.[6]

The need to simplify rate making procedure, particularly in the determination of fair value, must not lead to a neglect of other equally important considerations in choosing a new method of rate making. No rate making plan can be satisfactory in the long run unless it protects the legitimate interests of the community: the interest of the investors in utility securities and of the consumers of utility services. It is necessary, therefore, that the new rate making plan should assure to utility companies a net income that will attract the capital required for continued expansion of the utility industries. Rate making under the new plan should also be sufficiently responsive to changing economic conditions to prevent an undesirable divergence of utility rates from the costs of producing utility services.

The prudent investment method of valuation meets these tests in every respect. It is simple and definite, so that it facilitates administrative control of utility rates; and at the same time it assures to utility companies protection of their capital investment undertaken for the public convenience at the order of the rate making authority. There can be no greater stimulus to the economical provision of adequate utility capital than the assurance of the utilities commission that the investment, if prudently made, will be protected against the hazards of fortuitous price changes. At the same time, the continued retirement, replacement, and expansion of utility equipment would give considerable weight to the prices of recent years in a prudent investment valuation. Thus, the prudent investment method of determining fair value would induce continued provision of capital for utility enterprises, while maintaining a responsiveness of utility rates to changing costs of producing utility services.

The proposals for modifying the present method of determining fair rate of return that were submitted to the New York legislative commission do not meet all the tests of a desirable

[6] It will be apparent that a plan for fixing present value with the provision that future additions are to be valued at actual investment, prudently made, is an application of the split inventory method in which the division date is the time of the fixing of the initial value.

method of rate making. Unquestionably, the use of a fixed return equal to the actual cost of acquiring capital at the time the securities were issued would result in simplifying the present method of determining fair rate of return. But a fixed return would not be sufficiently sensitive to changing costs of producing utility services, and it would be objectionable on that account. Further, it is doubtful whether a fixed return would be conducive to investment in the common stock of utility enterprises. For if the dividend on common stock were fixed, the market price of the shares would fluctuate with every change in current interest rates. Thus, with a rise in interest rates it would be impossible to issue additional common stock except at a price below par. Nor would a large degree of fluctuation in the market price of common stock be attractive to those investors who are interested in the regularity and stability of income rather than in the speculative possibilities of utility securities.

The common stock basis for return would offer a simple method of determining fair rate of return, while maintaining stability in the price of utility securities, and a responsiveness of utility rates to changing costs of producing utility services. Under this method, rate schedules for utility companies would be designed to provide sufficient revenue to meet operating expenses and the capital charges for interest on bonds and dividends on preferred stock, and to permit that rate of dividends on common stock that will maintain the market price of the stock at par or at the price at which issue of the stock was authorized by the commission. This is substantially the plan that has been used successfully in Massachusetts (*Hearings,* pp. 753-831).

Granting the desirability of establishing the prudent investment basis for valuation and the common stock basis for return, it remains to be considered whether such a rate making plan can be established. It is doubtful whether the Constitution permits any rate making plan, other than the present rate making rule, to be used without the consent of the utility companies. This was recognized in the Donovan plan, and it was admitted as a contingency in the Bauer plan. It is necessary, therefore, to induce utility companies to agree to the use of the rate making plan proposed in this section. This can probably be done in the manner stated below.

The legislature should authorize the issue of new franchises to all utility companies that agree to the following rate making provisions. An initial valuation of the property of the public utility company is to be made by a valuation committee jointly selected by the company and the commission. Once determined and approved by the company and the commission, this initial fair value is not to be subject to later change because of price fluctuations. Additions and betterments after the initial valuation are to be valued at actual cost prudently made. Deductions for depreciation and retirement are to be determined from reserves accumulated for these purposes as shown by the accounts. Charges for interest on bonds and dividends on preferred stock are to be allowed as capital expenses. The fair return to common stockholders is to be fixed at the rate that will maintain the market value of the common stock of a representative utility company at par or at the price at which the commission authorized the issue. This fair rate of return is to be fixed annually by the commission, after a hearing, and it is to be the standard rate of return for that year for all utility companies managed with representative economy and efficiency. Deficiencies in the return for any given year are to be carried over and to be compensated in subsequent years.

Franchises providing for this new method of rate making are to be offered to all utility companies. Those that accept the franchises are to be assured of freedom from competition from publicly owned utility plants. The public is to be protected, however, by the reservation of the right to purchase the franchise and property of such utility companies by the state or the municipality at the rate base established by the commission under this plan. Utility companies that do not accept the new franchises as a basis for the regulation of their rates are to be subject to competition from publicly owned plants.

5. THE PROSPECT FOR THE NEW PLAN

There are two reasons for believing that this plan will induce nearly all utility companies to accept new franchises providing for the use of this new method of rate making. First, the rate making policy of the Massachusetts Commission, not far different from the proposed plan, has met with little objection from the utility companies of that state. Mr. Henry C. Atwill, head of the Massachusetts Department of Public Utilities, testified before the New York legislative commission that from 1885 to 1929 only four rate cases were appealed to the courts by the utilities of his state. They have permitted the use of the prudent investment method of determining fair value and the common stock basis for return not only because they have prospered under this rate making rule, but because they know that insistence on the rate making procedure in use in other states would induce the people of Massachusetts to undertake public ownership and operation of utilities (*Hearings,* pp. 755, 764).

A second reason for believing that utility companies would accept the proposed new franchises is that the rate making method for which it provides agrees with the practice of many leading utility companies and with the preference expressed by their executives. In the 1927 annual report of the American Telephone & Telegraph Co., Mr. Walter S. Gifford indicated that the common stock basis for return would be in harmony with the policy of that company.

The American Telephone & Telegraph Co. accepts its responsibility for a nationwide telephone service as a public trust. Its duty is to provide the American public with adequate, dependable and satisfactory telephone service at a reasonable cost. To attain this end, it is the policy of the company to pay only reasonable regular dividends, and for part of the new capital needed, to offer from time to time new stock to its stockholders on favorable terms, for it believes this method of financing will provide the money needed for the business cheaply and with more certainty in good times and bad than any other.

The safety of principal and regular dividends have been the compelling motives that have led to the widespread ownership of the stock of the company. . . . Extra or special dividends are entirely inconsistent with this aim and would be unsound. Earnings must, of course, be sufficient to permit the best possible telephone service at all times and to provide a reasonable payment to stockholders with an adequate margin to insure financial safety. Earnings in excess of the requirements will either be spent for the enlargement and the improvement of the service furnished, or the rates charged for the service reduced. This is fundamental in the policy of the management (*Report*, p. 389; *Hearings*, pp. 2793-95).

The railroads, the largest group of utilities operating under the present rate making rule, have expressed their preference for a rate making method that will provide stable income despite price fluctuations. Mr. Alfred P. Thom, counsel for the Association of Railway Executives, testifying before the House Committee on Interstate and Foreign Commerce, asked that rates be determined so that they will yield sufficient revenue to maintain the railroads in the sound financial condition necessary to meet the public requirement for service, with provision for accumulating a surplus in prosperity for use in depression.[7] The views expressed by Mr. Gifford and Mr. Thom are typical of the attitude of enlightened utility executives all over the country. The new rate making plan is entirely in harmony with this attitude on rate making.

The proposal for the issue of new franchises requiring the use of the prudent investment method of valuation and the common stock basis for return should be attractive to investors in utility securities. The interest they have in the present method of rate making is speculative at best, limited to the common stockholders in utility enterprises. The holders of bonds and preferred stocks, who provide the greater part of the capital invested in the utility industries, can have no reason for preferring a rate making method that results in a variable return from which they cannot gain and from which they can suffer loss. Even among common stockholders there are many who prefer the financial security of a moderate and fair return on their investment to the risk of a speculative return that fluctuates violently with changes in prices and interest rates. The recent depression has shown conclusively that the financial stability of the utility industries is endangered by the use of present methods of determining fair value and fair rate of return.

[7] *The New York Times*, February 21, 1932.

The proposed plan for bringing about a change in rate making methods is probably constitutional. The new franchise would constitute a contract specifying the use of a particular method of rate making. In the past, the Supreme Court has held that rates embodied in a contract are not subject to the constitutional test of yielding a fair rate of return on the fair value of the utility company's property. It would seem that the same reasoning applies to rate making methods established by contract. There is a possibility that the Supreme Court will hold that the legislature of a state cannot relinquish the right to regulate utility rates, although it is difficult to see how a franchise providing for a definite method of rate making by a state commission can be regarded as a surrender of the right of regulation. In fact, there is no great likelihood that the Supreme Court would disallow the new rate making plan if it were specified in franchises accepted by the utility companies. Rather, there is a possibility that a legislative act establishing the proposed rate making method, without the consent of the utility companies, would be held constitutional by the court. Three members of the Supreme Court have repeatedly urged that prudent investment valuation and the common stock or the capital cost basis for return are not in violation of constitutional guaranties. It is not too much to hope that a majority of the court may yet see the need for a revision of the present rate making rule.

Sufficient time has now elapsed since regulation of public utility rates was undertaken to determine finally what public policy requires. It is obvious that after forty years of development, the rate making method now commonly used is too complex, too dilatory, and too expensive to permit effective regulation of utility rates. Unless this unsatisfactory situation is speedily remedied, the policy of private operation and public regulation of utilities will have to be abandoned. The time is now particularly favorable for the establishment of a new rate making policy. It is to be hoped that the legislatures of the states, with the coöperation of the public utility companies and the public utilities commissions, will take positive steps to end the present chaos in rate making.

INDEX

ABILITY to pay, 110
Accounting, 20, 26, 83, 127, 131
Additional percentage, 59, 84. *See also*
  Appreciation, Corrective indices
Administrative problems, 26
Administrative rate making, 5
Alabama Public Service Commission,
  67
Allison, J. E., 17
American Electric Railway Associa-
  tion, 58
American Society of Civil Engineers,
  10, 44
American Telephone & Telegraph Co.,
  132
Appreciation, 18, 38, 59-61. *See also*
  Corrective indices
Approximate valuations, 42
Arizona Corporation Commission, 40
Arkansas Department of Public Utili-
  ties, 49
Ashland Water Co. (Wisc.), 82
Association of Railway Executives, 133
Atwill, H. C., 132
Average unit prices, advantages of, 56;
  attitude of courts toward, 55; attitude
  of utilities toward, 46, 57, 113; disadvantages of, 57, 88; fifteen-year,
  53; five-year, 44, 46-49, 77; four-
  year, 47; prewar use of, 44-46; replaced by corrective indices, 69; ten-
  year, 44, 49-53; three-year, 47;
  twenty-year, 53; two-year, 47; used
  in railroad valuation, 84; used with
  split inventory, 76; war construction
  and, 58

BALTIMORE street railway case, 108
Bauer, J., 24, 127
Bauer plan, 93, 127-128, 130
Bay State Street Railway Co. (Mass.),
  98
Bickley, J. H., 91
Bluefield Water Works & Improvement
  Co. (W. Va.), 87, 102
Bonbright, J. C., 87, 127
Bonds. *See* Securities.
Book cost. *See* Prudent investment
Brandeis, Justice, 20, 43, 86-87, 93,
  101, 102, 109

Brewer, Justice, 5
Brooklyn Borough Gas Co. (N. Y.),
  39, 47, 54, 77, 79
Brown, H. G., 122
Brundige, H. W., 40
Buck, S. J., 4
Built up value, 75, 77, 81, 88. *See also*
  Split inventory
Burdens of depression, 115
Burdens of war, 94, 95, 99
Bureau of Labor Statistics index num-
  bers, 60, 67, 70, 71, 113, 118
Butler, Justice, 55, 87, 102

CALIFORNIA Railroad Commission
  on average prices, 47; prudent in-
  vestment, 105; return, 107, 110; split
  inventory, 77; wartime return, 40
Cambridge Electric Light Co. (Mass.),
  108
Capital cost and fair return, 28-30, 38,
  91-93, 99, 102, 103, 121, 125, 128,
  130, 131. *See also* Corporate needs
Capital structure and fair return, 30-31
Capitalization. *See* Prudent investment
Cardozo, Justice, 116
Cedar Rapids Gas Co. (Ia.), 18
Chesapeake & Potomac Telephone Co.
  (Md.), 66, 69, 71, 114
Coal Prices, 33, 36
Coast Gas Co. (N. J.), 60, 70
Columbus Gas Light Co. (Ind.), 97
Commissions, bound by constitution, 4;
  bound by rate making rule, 8-9;
  emergency powers of, 33; estab-
  lished, 5; facilities for work of, 6.
  See also Alabama Public Service
  Commission, Arizona Corporation
  Commission, etc.
Committee on Interstate and Foreign
  Commerce, 133
Common law, 3
Common stock basis for return, 31,
  38, 92, 93, 99, 103, 116, 121, 125,
  130, 132, 134
Compensatory return. *See* Rate of re-
  turn
Competitive rate making, 3, 4
Conference of Governors and Mayors,
  34

Confiscation. *See* Rate of return
Congress, 4
Connecticut Public Utilities Commission, 40
Consolidated Gas Co. (N. Y.), 17, 18, 19, 38, 48, 54, 71
Constitutional rights, 4, 5, 7, 9, 12, 17, 18, 22, 35, 52, 82, 114, 134
Construction costs, 38, 50, 72, 73, 123
Consumers, 31, 39, 110, 129
Consumers' income, 22, 111
Contract plan, 127, 128
Cooke, M. L., 36, 49
Cooley, Professor, 44
Corporate needs, 35, 37, 97, 98, 103
Corrective indices, advantages of, 69, 113; additional percentage and, 59; attitude of courts toward, 65, 67-68; during depression, 113-15; future use of, 126; misuse of, 68; objections to, 72; used by federal courts, 63
Cost of producing utility services, 3, 4, 23-24, 122, 129
Courts. *See* Federal courts, State courts, Supreme Court

D AYTON-Goose Creek Railway Co., 102
Dayton Power & Light Co. (Ohio), 116
Deficiency in return, 131
Deflation. *See* Depression, Interest rates, Prices, Profits
Depreciation, 10, 13, 18, 26, 131
Depression, 4, 5, 6, 13, 21, 29, 45, 109-11
Des Moines Gas Co. (Ia.), 17
Discrimination, 3
District of Columbia Public Utilities Commission, 44, 77
Dividends, 30, 97, 98, 118. *See also* Common stock basis for return
Donovan, W. J., 127, 128, 130
Dozier, H. D., 92
Due process of law. *See* Constitutional rights
Duluth Street Railway Co. (Minn.), 66

E CONOMIC emergency. *See* Depression, War
Efficiency of management, 14, 15, 16, 97
Electric light and power industry, 20, 34, 50, 73

Elements of fair value. *See* Prudent investment, Reproduction cost
Elizabethtown Gas Light Co. (N. J.), 54, 100
Elizabethtown Water Co. (N. J.), 109
Emergency powers, 33, 36, 37
Emergency rate making, 37, 41, 111
Engineering News-Record index number, 63, 71, 72, 73, 113, 114
Equal protection of the law. *See* Constitutional rights
Equalization reserve, 128
Equipment, 10, 75
Equivalent service, 24
Expansion, 13, 16, 27

F AIR return. *See* Rate of return
Fair value, affects return, 13; cases in Supreme Court, 17; cost of determining, 35; factors to be considered in, 9-10; normal value, 38; proposed methods of determining, 126-31; required for rate making, 5; translator for, 114; unit prices and, 12; wartime methods of determining, 32. *See also* Average prices, Corrective indices, Prudent investment, Reproduction cost, Split inventory, Valuation
Farrington, Judge, 65
Federal courts on average prices, 54; burdens of war, 41, 95; corrective indices, 63-64, 67-68, 114; current prices, 62; deficient return, 94; prudent investment, 105; reproduction cost, 106; return, 13, 100, 108, 109, 116, 117; split inventory, 79, 80, 82, 85; temporary rates, 112
Federal courts, cases in, Ashland Water Co. (Wisc.), 82; Cambridge Electric Light Co. (Mass.), 108; Consolidated Gas Co. (N. Y.), 54; Duluth Street Railway Co. (Minn.), 66; Elizabethtown Water Co. (N. J.), 109; Fort Worth Gas Co. (Tex.), 108; Galveston Electric Co. (Tex.), 64, 86, 101; Georgia Railway & Power Co. (Ga.), 66, 87; Greencastle Water Works Co. (Ind.), 108; Houston Electric Co. (Tex.), 63; Indianapolis Water Co. (Ind.), 55, 102; Joplin Gas Co. (Mo.), 63; Kings County Lighting Co. (N. Y.), 94; Maryland telephone company, 66, 114; Minneapolis Gas Light Co.

(Minn.), 65; Mobile Gas Co. (Ala.), 67; Monroe Gas Light & Fuel Co. (Mich.), 68; New York & Queens Gas Co. (N. Y.), 94; New York Telephone Co. (N. Y.), 80; Pacific Gas & Electric Co. (Calif.), 105; Potomac Electric Power Co. (D. C.), 79; St. Joseph Railway, Light, Heat & Power Co. (Mo.), 79; St. Louis & O'Fallon Railway Co., 85; Southern California Telephone Co. (Calif.), 105; Springfield Gas & Electric Co. (Mo.), 63; Toledo Railways & Light Co. (Ohio), 41; West Palm Beach Water Co. (Fla.), 116; Wisconsin-Minnesota Light & Power Co. (Minn.), 64; Worcester Electric Light Co. (Mass.), 106

Federal operation, 33, 62

Financial stability, 110, 112, 133

Fixed return, 93, 121, 128, 130

Formula for rate making, 12, 13, 16, 17, 120. *See also* Uniform methods of rate making

Fort Worth Gas Co. (Tex.), 108

Franchise plan, 130, 131, 133

Franchise value, 10

GALVESTON Electric Co. (Tex.), 64, 86, 101

Gas industry, 20, 34, 72, 73

Georgia Public Service Commission, 42, 87

Georgia Railway & Power Co. (Ga.), 42, 66, 87, 102

Gifford, W. S., 132, 133

Goddard, E. C., 20, 87

Going concern value, 10

Gold, N., 24

Good will value, 10

Granger movement, 4

Green Bay Water Co. (Wisc.), 80

Greencastle Water Works Co. (Ind.), 108

Grunsky, C. E., 123

HADLEY, A. T., 4

Hand, Judge L., 20, 54, 55, 71

Harlan, Justice, 17

Hartford street railway case, 40

Hayes, H. V., 17

Historical cost. *See* Prudent investment

Holmes, Justice, 18, 86, 93, 101

Home Telephone Co. (Ind.), 49

Houston Electric Co. (Tex.), 63

Hughes, Chief Justice, 18, 39, 47, 54, 77, 79

Hutcheson, Judge, 63, 64

IDAHO Public Utilities Commission, 14

Illinois Bell Telephone Co. (Ill.), 118

Illinois Commerce Commission on average prices, 47, 49; corporate needs, 99; normal return, 95-96; rate of return, 107; split inventory, 77; valuation conferences, 49

Improvident investment, 18

Income of consumers, 22, 111

Index numbers, Bureau of Labor Statistics, 60, 67; construction costs, 72, 73; cost of living, 71; during depression, 113, 118; retail prices, 71, 72; special indices, 70; wholesale prices, 71, 72. *See also* Corrective indices

Indiana Bell Telephone Co. (Ind.), 97

Indiana Public Service Commission on average prices, 48, 52, 53, 58; normal return, 96-97; prudent investment, 48; reproduction cost, 105; return, 103; return during depression, 115; split inventory, 77

Indianapolis Water Co. (Ind.), 52, 55, 102

Inflation, 5, 29, 49. *See also* Interest rates, Prices, Prosperity, War

Intangibles, 10, 11, 75

Interest rates, during depression, 29, 110, 115; fluctuations of, 5, 6, 13, 20-21, 29, 94, 107, 115; investors and, 30; and rate of return, 14, 29, 97; during prosperity, 94, 107; table of, 94, 107, 115; during war, 29, 38, 94

Interstate Commerce Commission, 4, 45, 51, 83-85, 102

Inventory for valuation, 10, 11, 26, 83

Investment. *See* Expansion, Prudent investment

Investors, 28, 29, 129, 133

Iroquois Natural Gas Co. (N. Y.), 79

JOPLIN Gas Co. (Mo.), 63

Judicial review, 5. *See also* Federal courts, State courts, Supreme Court

Just compensation. *See* Constitutional rights

KINGS County Lighting Co. (N. Y.), 94

LAND valuation, 10, 11, 75, 83
Legal questions, 22, 23, 127, 128, 134
Legislative rate making, 4, 5
Legislatures and rate making, 5, 8, 125, 127, 134
Lincoln Gas & Electric Light Co. (Neb.), 95, 101
Litigation, 5, 12, 21, 26, 42, 119, 120
Location of industry, 122
Lockport Light, Heat & Power Co. (N. Y.), 78
Lynchburg Traction & Light Co. (Va.), 61

McADOO, W. G., 34, 37, 97
McReynolds, Justice, 101
Maine Public Utilities Commission, 50, 107, 110
Maintenance of service, 34, 35
Maryland Public Service Commission on corporate needs, 37, 98; rate of return, 108; split inventory, 77
Maryland telephone case, 66, 69, 71, 114
Massachusetts Commissioners of the Department of Public Utilities on common stock basis for return, 92, 117; corporate needs, 98; rate making policy, 132; rate of return, 99
Massachusetts plan, 130
Maximum original cost, 83
Michigan Board of Tax Commissioners, 44
Michigan Public Utilities Commission, 68, 70, 110
Milwaukee Electric Railway & Light Co. (Wisc.), 80
Minimum valuations, 42
Minneapolis Gas Light Co. (Minn.), 65
Minnesota Railroad and Warehouse Commission, 40
Minnesota rate cases, 11, 18
Missouri Public Service Commission on average prices, 61; corrective indices, 62, 63; high prices, 39; prudent investment, 61; rate of return, 14, 107; split inventory, 77, 86; temporary rates, 112; wartime valuation, 36

Mobile Gas Light Co. (Ala.), 67
Monroe Gas Light & Fuel Co. (Mich.), 68, 70
Montpelier & Barre Light & Power Co. (Vt.), 51
Mt. Vernon water case, 78
Munger, Judge, 65
Munn v. Illinois, 4

NASH, L. R., 73
National Electric Railway Commission, 34
Natural gas industry, 15
Nebraska State Railway Commission, 39
Nevada Public Service Commission, 15
New Hampshire Public Service Commission, 77
New Jersey Board of Public Utility Commissioners on appreciation, 60; average prices, 60; corrective indices, 70; split inventory, 77; valuation conferences, 49
New York Commission on Revision of the Public Service Commissions Law, 6, 93, 126-29
New York Department of Public Service, Public Service Commission on burdens of war, 99; common stock basis for return, 116; corporate needs, 98; emergency rate making, 111; index numbers, 113; rate of return, 99, 107; split inventory, 77-80
New York Department of Public Service, Transit Commission, 78
New York Interurban Water Co. (N. Y.), 78
New York Public Service Commission: first district, 78; second district, 78. See also New York Department of Public Service
New York State Railways (N. Y.), 80
New York Telephone Co. (N. Y.), 80
New York Transit Commission, 78
Normal appreciation, 60, 70
Normal rate of return, 38, 39, 94, 95-97, 99, 103
Normal value, 38, 39, 46, 50
North Carolina rate making law, 8
North Carolina Utilities Commission, 113
North Dakota Board of Railroad Commissioners, 45

O'FALLON case, 85
Ohio Public Utilities Commission, 77, 110
Operating expenses, 8, 22, 27, 33, 34
Oregon Public Utilities Commissioner, 77, 115
Original conditions of construction, 17, 24
Original cost. *See* Prudent investment
Overheads. *See* Intangibles

PACIFIC Gas & Electric Co. (Calif.), 105
Past earnings, 16, 128, 131
Pennsylvania Public Utility Commission on average prices, 45, 48, 50, 52; rate of return, 107, 115; reproduction cost, 52; valuation conferences, 48
Potomac Electric Power Co. (D. C.), 79
Prendergast, W. A., 6, 126
Prendergast plan, 126
Present cost. *See* Reproduction cost
Present value rule, 18, 82
Price level. *See* Index numbers, Prices
Prices, abnormal, 39; coal, 33, 36; current, 53; fluctuations in, 5, 6, 13, 20-21, 28, 29, 56; future, 51, 62, 64; postwar, 51, 57; rates and, 110; trend of, 60, 70; reproduction cost and, 112; wartime, 33, 38. *See also* Wage rates
Prima facie valuation, 36, 42
Private operation, 7, 134
Procedure for rate making, and average prices, 56; complex and expensive, 29; dilatory, 35; corrective indices and, 69; during depression, 118; objections to present, 27; and split inventory, 75, 81, 88; unsatisfactory, 120; in wartime, 43, 59
Productive resources, 23-24, 122
Profiteering, 39
Profits in competitive industry, 101, 105, 107, 115, 116, 119
Property used and useful, 9, 10, 11
Prosperity, 29, 45, 105-9
Prudent investment, advantages of, 26-28, 129; attitude of Supreme Court toward, 134; basis for proposed uniform method of rate making, 121, 127; capital cost and, 28; changing costs of production and, 123; commissions prefer, 48, 120; consideration required, 8, 12, 83; and constitutional rights, 22, 23; and corporate needs, 38; current prices and, 124; during depression, 111; disadvantages of, 122; economic aspects of, 26-28; investors and, 27; legal theory of, 23; method of determining, 26; price fluctuations and, 21, 22; security issues and, 38; and stability of return, 28; and split inventory, 75, 89, 90; and wartime valuation, 42
Public interest, 3
Public ownership, 7, 131, 132
Public purchase, 131
Purchasing power, 25, 55, 71, 110

QUEENS gas case, 94

RACINE Water Co. (Wisc.), 80
Railroads, 20, 33, 44, 83-85, 133
Rate base. *See* Fair value
Rate making, administrative, 6; competitive, 3, 4; legislative, 4, 5; problems, 5-7; rule, 5, 6, 8, 16, 18; uniform methods of, 16; unit prices and, 12; unsettled questions of, 9; wartime methods of, 6, 7, 33-34, 37, 41. *See also* Average prices, Corrective indices, Fair value, Procedure for rate making, Prudent investment, Rate of return, Reproduction cost, Split inventory
Rate of return, base to which applied, 91; capital cost and, 28-29, 31; capital structure and, 30-31; compensatory, 19; in competitive industry, 31; controversies on, 29; in depression, 114-15, 117; dividends and, 97; and emergency rates, 111; excessive, 30-31; factors affecting, 14; interest rates and, 21, 91; past earnings and, 16; profits and, 115; proposed methods of determining, 128; in prosperity, 107-8, 119; variability of, 29; wartime methods of determining, 32. *See also* Capital cost, Common stock basis for return, Corporate needs, Normal return, Stable return, Standard rate of return
Rates, comparative, 15; consumers' income and, 22, 111; emergency, 111;

inadequate, 5; prices and, 21-23; schedules of, 13
Raver, P. J., 73
Reasonable appreciation, 71
Reasonable worth, 8, 39, 109-11
Recapture of excess earnings, 102
Regulation, 3, 7, 134
Reproduction cost, attitude of courts, 121; advantages of, 23-25; and average prices, 44, 56; consideration required, 8, 63, 83; constitutional rights and, 17; during depression, 112; disadvantages of, 23-25; dominant consideration given to, 105, 106; economic aspects of, 22-25; and fair value, 64; investors and, 25; legal theory of, 23; method of determining, 25; normal, 40, 50; prices and, 21, 22; and wartime valuation, 41
Richberg, D. R., 92
Rigidity of rates, 27
Risk, 14, 15, 28, 30
Rockford City Traction Co. (Ill.), 96
Roosevelt, Franklin D., 125, 127
Rosenberry, Judge, 82
Ruggles, C. O., 91

St. JOSEPH Railway, Light, Heat & Power Co. (Mo.), 79
St. Louis & O'Fallon Railway Co., 85
San Diego Land & Town Co. (Calif.), 17, 18
San Joaquin & Kings River Canal & Irrigation Co. (Calif.), 17
Securities, 25, 28, 38, 91
Single sum value, 84
Sliding scale, 36
Smyth v. Ames, and corporate needs, 37; elements of value prescribed in, 12; modification in rule proposed, 127; procedure conforms to rule of, 16; and reasonable worth, 109; rule of, 8; and split inventory, 89; uniform methods of rate making and, 20; on valuation, 17; and wartime rate making, 41, 42
South Carolina Public Service Commission, 114
Southern Bell Telephone & Telegraph Co. (N. C.), 113
Southern California Telephone Co. (Calif.), 105

Southwestern Bell Telephone Co. (Mo.), 20, 43, 62, 93, 101, 113
Speculation, 28, 82, 119
Split inventory, abandoned, 82; attitude of courts toward, 78-80, 85; advantages of, 88; average prices and, 76; built up value, 75; classified inventory, 75; defined, 75; division date, 76; Interstate Commerce Commission uses, 85-87; land valuation and, 75; misuse of, 86, 88; New York uses, 78-80; proposed use of, 126, 129; purpose of, 75, 77, 88; Wisconsin uses, 80-82
Spring Water Co. (Penna.), 49
Springfield Gas & Electric Co. (Ill.), 96
Springfield Gas & Electric Co. (Mo.), 63
Stable return, 25, 71. See also Fixed return
Standard rate of return, 19, 91, 95-96, 104, 108, 117, 131
State courts on average prices, 54, 60; burdens of war, 94; corrective indices, 61; emergency rate making, 100, 111; normal return, 96, 97; rate of return, 100; return during depression, 116, 117; split inventory, 78-79, 82, 85
State courts, cases in, Bluefield Water Works & Improvement Co. (W. Va.), 87; Brooklyn Borough Gas Co. (N. Y.), 39, 47; Columbus Gas Light Co. (Ind.), 97; Elizabethtown Gas Light Co. (N. J.), 54, 100; Iroquois Natural Gas Co. (N. Y.), New York Interurban Water Co. (N. Y.), 78; New York State Railways (N. Y.), 80; Southwestern Bell Telephone Co. (Mo.), 86; Springfield Gas & Electric Co. (Ill.), 96; United Railways & Electric Co. of Baltimore (Md.), 108; Waukesha Gas & Electric Co. (Wisc.), 82
Stocks and bonds. See Securities
Stone, Justice, 88, 102, 114
Street railways, 20, 34, 72, 73
Supreme Court on capital cost and return, 134; constitutional guaranties, 4; contract rates, 134; corrective indices, 114; current prices, 53; fair value, 16-17; fixed return, 93; formulas for rate making, 120; juris-

diction, 9; land value, 11; prudent investment, 18, 134; rate making rule, 5; rate of return, 13, 19, 100-101, 108; reproduction cost, 18, 56; return during depression, 116, 118; split inventory, 85-86; uniform methods of rate making, 20; wartime return, 95

Supreme Court, cases in, Bluefield Water Works & Improvement Co., 87, 102; Cedar Rapids Gas Co., 18; Chesapeake & Potomac Telephone Co., 114; Consolidated Gas Co., 17; Dayton Power & Light Co., 116; Galveston Electric Co., 64, 86, 101; Georgia Railway & Power Co., 102; Illinois Bell Telephone Co., 118; Indianapolis Water Co., 56; Lincoln Gas & Electric Co., 95, 101; Minnesota rate cases, 18; *Munn v. Illinois*, 4; St. Louis & O'Fallon Railway Co., 85; San Diego Land & Town Co., 17; San Joaquin & Kings River Canal & Irrigation Co., 17; *Smyth v. Ames*, 8; Southwestern Bell Telephone Co., 62, 86, 101; Texas railroad rate cases, 5; United Railways & Electric Co. of Baltimore, 108; West Ohio Gas Co., 118

Sutherland, Justice, 108

Swayze, Judge, 100

TELEPHONE industry, 15, 20, 33, 72, 73, 114

Temporary deficiency of return, 94-95, 111

Temporary rate making, 111. *See also* Emergency rate making

Temporary valuations, 36, 41, 81

Tennessee Railroad and Public Utilities Commission, 110

Tentative valuations, 42, 81

Texas railroad rate cases, 5

Thom, A. P., 133

Toledo Railways & Light Co. (Ohio), 41, 95

Tompkins, Judge, 79

Transit Commission of New York, 78

Transportation Act of 1920, 83-84, 102

UNIFORM methods of rate making, 16, 20, 21, 22, 121. *See also* Formula for rate making

Unit prices, 10, 12, 26, 44, 83, 113. *See also* Average unit prices

United Fuel Gas Co. (W. Va.), 112

United Railways & Electric Co. of Baltimore (Md.), 108

Utah Public Service Commission, 94, 112

Utica Gas & Electric Co. (N. Y.), 79

Utilities. *See* Electric light and power industry, Gas industry, etc.

VALUATION, conferences on, 48, 49, 131; expense of, 27; informal methods of, 42; objects of wartime, 59; reduction of, 49, 50; wartime methods of, 41-42. *See also* Average unit prices, Corrective indices, Fair value, Prudent investment, Reproduction cost, Split inventory

Valuation Act of 1913, 44, 83

Valuation Brief of 1915, 45, 51

Value of money. *See* Purchasing power

Vermont Public Service Commission, 51

Virginia Railway & Power Co. (Va.), 60

Virginia State Corporation Commission, 60, 61

WAGE rates, 33, 83, 112

War, burdens of, 38; boards, 33; construction costs during, 38; emergency, 95; fair value in time of, 41; interest rates during, 29, 38; objects of rate making in time of, 33-34, 89; rate making rule and, 41; sacrifices of, 40; valuation methods developed in time of, 32. *See also* Average unit prices, Corrective indices, Normal return, Normal value, Split inventory

War Finance Corporation, 97, 99

Washington Department of Public Works, 39, 115

Water works, 15, 20, 72, 73

Waukesha Gas & Electric Co. (Wisc.), 82

West Ohio Gas Co. (Ohio), 118

West Palm Beach Water Co. (Fla.), 116

West Virginia Public Service Commission, 58, 87, 112

Wilson, Woodrow, 34, 37, 97, 99

Wisconsin-Minnesota Light & Power Co. (Minn.), 64

Wisconsin Public Service Commission on average prices, 45; common stock basis for return, 117; corporate needs, 100; emergency rates, 111; rate of return in depression, 110; split inventory, 77, 80-82

Wisconsin railroad valuation, 44

Worcester Electric Light Co. (Mass.), 106

YARDSTICK, 15

Yield on utility bonds, 94, 104, 107, 114, 115

York Water Co. (Penna.), 52

www.ingramcontent.com/pod-product-compliance
Lightning Source LLC
Chambersburg PA
CBHW030653270326
41929CB00007B/349